# Man From A Far Country

*By the same author*

LONGFORD
BLESSINGS

For my aunts
Betty, Mollie and Josephine

# Man From A Far Country

*A Portrait of Pope John Paul II*

by

## MARY CRAIG

**HODDER AND STOUGHTON**
LONDON SYDNEY AUCKLAND TORONTO

ACKNOWLEDGMENTS
The Author and Publishers are grateful to Popperfoto for permission to
use the photographs in the text.


British Library Catologuing in Publication Data
Craig, Mary, b.1928
Man From A Far Country
1. JP2, *Pope*
2. Popes –Biography
I. Title
262;.13;0924       BX1378.5

ISBN 0-340-24235-3

O highlander, do you not grieve
for the land that gave you birth,
for the forests of spruce and the meadows,
and the streams of running silver?

O highlander, do you not grieve?


*Góralu, czy ci nie żal*
*Odchodzić od stron ojczystych,*
*Swierkowych lasów i hal*
*I tych potoków srebrzystych?*

*Góralu, czy ci nie żal?*

*Polish folk song*

# Pronunciation of Polish words

Polish proper names have been kept to a minimum.
The ones which recur most frequently are:

Wojtyla (Voy-tĭ-wa)
Wyszynski (Vish-ĭnsky)
Czestochowa (Chensto-hŏva)

If the reader can keep in mind that:

*c* is usually (though not invariably) pronounced *ts*
*ch* = kh (as in loch)
*cz* = ch (as in church)
*j* = y
*rz* = zh
*sz* = sh
*szcz* = sh-ch
*w* = v
*i* = ee
*y* = ĭ

both he and she may survive the obstacle course without too much difficulty.

# Contents

# Acknowledgments

To many friends in Cracow who shall be nameless.

To *Jessica Gatty,* (Sister Jessica of the Assumption Order) for her fluent Polish, her invaluable assistance as interpreter in Cracow, and for translating articles from *Tygodnik Powszechny.*

To *Olgierd Stepan,* who helped with advice and information and who went through the original MS with a fine-tooth comb.

To *Archbishop Worlock, Mgr George Leonard* and *Mr Patrick Keegan.* And also to the librarian at the Catholic Library in Westminster.

To *St Paul Publications,* of Slough who have the exclusive right to publish *Sign of Contradiction* in the English language, but who generously gave me permission to use extracts from the Italian version (*Segno di Contraddizione*) in my own translation, since theirs was not ready when this book went to print.

To *Hutchinsons,* for permission to use material from *Easter Vigil and Other Poems* by Karol Wojtyla, translated by Jerzy Peterkiewicz, 1979.

I must also acknowledge my debt to the following newspapers and periodicals for the issues which appeared at the time of Pope John Paul II's election: *Catholic Herald, Daily Telegraph, Documentations Catholiques Internationales, Domenica del Corriere, Economist, Epoca, Famiglia Cristiana, Informations Catholiques Internationales, Jours de France, Le Monde, Newsweek, Observer, Oggi, Osservatore Romano, Paris Match, Spectator, Sunday Times, Tablet, Il Tempo, Time* and *The Times.*

# Foreword

By His Eminence Cardinal Basil Hume

It is with genuine pleasure that I write this Foreword to Mary Craig's biography of Pope John Paul II. This book is a very readable account of the life of Karol Wojtyla up to his election to the papacy – but it is also far more. With great skill, the new Pope's personal story has been interwoven with national, political and social events in Poland and in Europe. Considerable research is evident throughout, much of it carried out in person in Poland. I am happy to know that English-speaking people will be able to discover in this book something of the character of Karol Wojtyla and some of the influences that have helped to prepare him for the burden of the papacy. Few will read it unmoved. At the same time, I hope that many will come to appreciate anew Poland and its courageous people.

Basil Hume.

Archbishop of Westminster
January, 1979

# Author's Introduction

A FEW DAYS AFTER the election of Cardinal Karol Wojtyla as John Paul II and two days before his installation in Rome, I went to Cracow. A book was wanted quickly, and there was no time to waste. So, dumping my suitcase, I set off in pursuit of what I could find.

'Which Wojtyla do you want me to talk about?' asked an old friend of the new Pope, looking more than slightly exasperated. 'Wojtyla the priest? Wojtyla the Church leader? the poet? the philosopher? the actor? the student hero? the friend of the poor? the country-lover? the contemplative? the sportsman? It may take several months, but ... where would you like to begin?'

I wish I could have stayed much longer, since even in a few days I learned enough to understand that Karol Wojtyla, Pope John Paul II, was not only a good and holy man, but a very rare and exceptional human being.

# 1

# A Week That Made History

ON THE EVENING OF Monday October 16th, at 18h.18 precisely, one hundred thousand people waiting on St Peter's Square saw the white smoke rising from the makeshift chimney of the Sistine Chapel. It was the end of the second day of waiting to know who would succeed the Pope of thirty-three days, Albino Luciani, Pope John Paul I. There was a yell of excitement and a burst of applause as everyone rushed to get as near as possible to the central balcony of St Peter's Basilica from where the announcement would be made.

Just under half an hour later, there was more applause, as the lights went on in the great hall, the window above the balcony opened slowly and Cardinal Pericle Felici stepped forward.

'I announce to you a great joy,' he intoned in the time-honoured formula for announcing the election of Popes. 'HABEMUS PAPAM' – we have a Pope. The crowd roared with relief and approval, then relapsed into expectant silence. The procedure, the words were established, immutable. Then came the first hint of the unexpected – the name – CAROLUM. Surely it could not be Confalonieri, Dean of the College of Cardinals, and aged eighty-five. If not him, who else was Carolum – Carlo? The thoughts of the crowd did not stray beyond the confines of Italy. Then, the big shock, the strange, unpronounceable name that took the crowd's breath away, and changed the face of the Papacy for the

foreseeable future. WOJTYLA. Who? *Chi è*? The crowd had
not the faintest idea. He might have been anyone, and for a
few seconds the people in the Square forbore to cheer.
Vietnamese? African? Slovak? Felici went on with the
Latin while they continued to speculate . . . who has taken
the name of John Paul II – *'qui sibi nomen imposuit Joan-
nem Paulum Secundum'*. The crowd cheered then, still
bemused but glad that the new Pope, whoever he was, had
taken the name of the gentle predecessor who had died so
suddenly after so brief a reign. And as it cheered, the crowd
pulled itself out of its astonishment and began to search the
special issue of the Vatican newspaper, *Osservatore
Romano*, which carried photographs of all the Cardinals
who had gone into the Conclave to elect a successor to St
Peter. Soon there were shouts of *'Ecco. È il Polacco.'* (Here
he is; it's the Pole.) The Cardinals, as *Time* magazine later
so aptly put it, 'had done not merely the unexpected but the
unthinkable'. After 455 years of Italian Popes, they had
swept aside tradition, and shown more imagination and
courage than anyone had thought to give them credit for.
They had chosen the first Polish Pope in the history of the
Roman Catholic Church, the first to come from Eastern
Europe, and certainly the first Pope to come from a nation
under Communist rule. What is more he was the youngest
Pope, at a mere fifty-eight, for more than a century. The
possibilities for the future were mind-boggling.

And now, here he was, Cardinal Wojtyla of Cracow,
Pope John Paul II. At 19h.22 he appeared on the balcony,
and the crowd, who may indeed have seen him many times
striding through the streets of Rome, now for the first time
took in the craggy features and broad cheekbones of the
Slav; the face full of quiet strength, though lined with past
suffering; the eyes clear and humorous. His audience
waited, expecting the traditional blessing, *Urbi et Orbi*, (to
the Church and the World) in Latin. Instead, breaking with
protocol (and shocking many of the Vatican officials
around him), he addressed them in a ringing voice, in a

fluent and barely-accented Italian. And immediately won their hearts.

'Praised be Jesus Christ,' he began, and the crowd roared back as one, 'Praised for evermore.' The voice went on, firm and compelling:

> *Carissimi fratelli e sorelle* – dearly beloved brothers and sisters, we are all still saddened by the death of our beloved Pope John Paul I and so the Cardinals have called for a new Bishop of Rome. They have called him from a far-away country, far-away and yet close, because of our communion in the traditions of the Church. I was afraid to accept that responsibility, yet I do so in a spirit of obedience to the Lord and total faithfulness to Mary our most holy Mother.

An official, horrified by this use of the vernacular, tried to shush him. 'Basta,' he implored. 'Enough.'

But Wojtyla, his voice breaking slightly with emotion, went on to win the crowd completely:

> I do not know if I can express myself well enough in your – no, *our*, Italian tongue. If I make mistakes, you will have to correct me.

It was a gesture towards them, and the crowd knew it and loved him for it. The applause that followed the blessing was tumultuous. Afterwards, it was said that they applauded him more than if he had been an Italian. 'He may be a foreigner, but he speaks our language,' said a woman in the Square. 'Why shouldn't we have a foreign Pope?' asked a Rome cabbie. 'After all, St Peter was one.'

\*       \*       \*

Meanwhile, about a thousand miles away, in Wojtyla's home town of Cracow, the first reaction was stupefied disbelief, the second an explosion of joy. Many heard it on the radio, thought they had misheard the name, and switched over to television for confirmation or disproof. Within minutes, thousands of telephones were ringing non-stop, as Cracovians rang friends and complete strangers in a kind of frenzy. 'Have you heard? Wojtyla's Pope!' Callers in their haste didn't even bother to identify themselves before ringing off and dialling another number. News spread like a bush-fire on Cracow's lumbering trams, in restaurants and late-opening shops, in cinemas, churches and along the streets. As crowds began to pour into the streets and on to the market place, smiling, laughing, singing, shouting, people were throwing their arms around everyone they met, hugging them, saying, 'It's impossible, unbelievable,' or 'Are you quite sure it's really true?' A doctor, on his way out to the street, received a phone call from a patient, a professor at the University and a long-time atheist: 'I had to ring', he shouted excitedly, 'I'm so full of emotion I've got to unload it on somebody.'

One girl student told a BBC reporter: 'We were in a hall of residence, one of the largest of the University, and when the news that the Cardinal had been elected Pope came over the loudspeakers there was such a roar of joy that the walls began to shake.' Other students, Marxist as well as Catholic, echoed her excitement: 'When I heard he had been chosen I felt such joy that I simply ran out into the street. I happened to run into a friend, we threw our arms around each other and there was a feeling of something like regained dignity. People seemed to be holding their heads up higher.' 'People were crying, although they were very happy, shouting for the Pope, for Poland. Wojtyla, well, he's such a personality, some people were saying, "Well, it's incredible," and they were also saying, "What shall we do now without him?"'[1]

Mass was said in the Church of St Mary (the Mariacki, with the world-famous altar-triptych by Wit Stwosz) at ten o'clock, and at midnight Mass was offered in a packed

Cathedral. Nowhere in Cracow is one out of sight of a church, and from the market place there are half a dozen within a hundred yards or so. Zygmunt, the largest bell in Poland, tolled out from the Cathedral, inviting the people of Cracow to give thanks for the news. They flocked willingly to the churches. Most of them felt the need to pray. The students for the most part streamed to their own church of St Anne, which normally closes its doors at nine, but on that Monday stayed open all night. Mass was said there too at midnight, and the church was packed to the doors, 'just as though it was Christmas'. 'The people were very concentrated,' said a girl student. 'There was absolute silence during the readings, and the singing was very strong, much stronger than usual. What I noticed was that people were tremendously moved, many of them cried, some of them laughed. The Poles are a very emotional people.'

No one went to bed that night. Young and old stayed in the Rynek Glowny, the historic market place which many say is the most beautiful in Europe, with its enchanting medieval Cloth Hall (the Sukiennice), and the splendid Gothic and Renaissance churches which surround it. 'The drawing-room', they call it in Cracow, and in the daytime it is ablaze with flower-stalls and a-flutter with pigeons, while the townsfolk gather in groups under the arches of the Sukiennice. This evening the square was floodlit, and all night long the crowd swayed and seethed, making emotional impromptu speeches, singing religious and national songs (often one and the same), reverting again and again to what often seems like an alternative national anthem – '*Sto Lat, sto lat, niech zyje zyje nam*' – the Polish equivalent of 'For he's a jolly good fellow'.

Students had already torn up cloth into strips to make streamers in the Vatican colours of yellow and white, as well as the Polish national colours of red and white. They even managed to fashion two full-size flags in both sets of colours. One of them they draped triumphantly across the statue of Mickiewicz, the great Polish poet and patriot, which stands in the market square. They carried the other flag in procession down Bracka Street and into the Street of the Franciscans (the Franciszkanska), where they laid it in front of their Cardinal's former residence. That particular moment was more bitter-sweet than the others.

\*    \*    \*

In Warsaw, earlier that same evening, Kazimierz Kakol, the Polish Minister for Church Affairs (not noted for his enthusiasm for the Church), was discussing the Conclave with a group of visiting journalists. Kakol expressed the hope that whoever was elected would continue the *Ostpolitik* of Paul VI, the policy of *rapprochement* with the Communist countries, which was frowned on by many Cardinals, its continuation therefore by no means assured. Conversation was relaxed. 'Now if they should happen to elect a Polish Pope,' he joked, 'I'll buy you all champagne.' General laughter, but ten minutes later, a rueful Kakol was pouring out champagne for his guests.

Throughout Warsaw the church bells rang out, Te Deums were being sung, and people were overcome with joy. 'It was as though our hearts stopped beating for a moment,' commented a Warsaw engineer. The initial television announcement on the seven-thirty news programme had been brief, stiff with official caution, but before long people began ringing the TV studios to complain. The next news programme made the Election the main item and let it run for ten minutes.

Official reaction was muted, uncertain, hovering between pride and dismay. (In Moscow and in other Communist-bloc capitals, reaction was positively lukewarm. Most of them failed to break the news for several hours, and then gave it cursory mention, without comment.) In Warsaw, an urgent meeting of the Party's *politburo* immediately following the announcement led to the despatch of a cordial message to the new Pope from the

President of the Polish People's Republic, Mr Henryk Jablonski, the Prime Minister, Mr Piotr Jaroszewicz, and, most important of all, the Party leader, Mr Edward Gierek. It ran as follows:

> The significant decision by the Conclave of Cardinals has caused great satisfaction in Poland. On the papal throne – for the first time in history – a son of the Polish nation is sitting.
>
> A nation warmly promoting co-operation and friendship between all peoples, a nation which has visibly contributed to the development of human culture.
>
> We are convinced that the further development of relations between the Polish People's Republic and the Holy See will continue to serve those important tasks.[2]

At the same time, the Government seemed to embark on a policy of give and take: give with one hand and take with the other. They issued directives to the Party-controlled Press that no photograph of the Pope was to be wider than one column, no headline on a papal story wider than two columns. On the Tuesday the Press was cautious, reflecting the uncertainty of its masters, but also optimistic, expressing hopes for a continuing thaw in relations with the Vatican. Warsaw's daily newspaper, *Życie Warszawy* (Warsaw Life), carried a picture of the former Cardinal (regulation size) with the feeble comment that the election had been received 'with obvious interest'. The Communist paper, *Trybuna Ludu* (Tribune of the People), published a report from Rome and a brief non-committal statement by a government spokesman, but prudently refrained from comment. (Later on in the week, this initial bashfulness was translated into a reasonable enthusiasm.)

The Catholic Press, both real and so-called, fared better. The whole front page of the daily paper, *Słowo Powszechne* (Universal Word), run by the subserviently pro-Government Pax group (which is generally mistrusted by both hierarchy and people), carried detailed election reports, the text of some of the Holy Father's speeches, and pictures of the Pope with Cardinal Wyszynski. The edition was sold out by seven o'clock next morning, with people ready to pay many times the cover price for it. The editor of the weekly Catholic paper, *Tygodnik Powszechny,* published in Cracow with the support and approval of Wojtyla, was less fortunate. He begged for a double ration of newsprint to celebrate the unique occasion (newsprint is strictly controlled by the State), but was refused. Only after what *The Times* called 'a long, screaming, tearful conversation' with the Central Committee in Warsaw did he wring a reluctant permission for an extra 15,000 copies on top of the usual 40,000 print run. (One sentence and one photograph were censored.) Its immediate sell-out was a foregone conclusion. Copies of this issue were so prized that in some villages they were being displayed behind glass on the walls of churches and municipal buildings. It was reported that copies were changing hands at astronomical prices – 300 zlotys instead of the usual six.

But, however grudging the Government's encouragement of the nation's runaway enthusiasm, it did make two important and unprecedented concessions (though it is probable that if they had not, the people might have rioted). Over two thousand visas were issued for those who wanted to and could afford to go to Rome for the installation ceremony; and it was agreed that the whole service would be transmitted live by Polish television. The fares to Rome were prohibitively high (the equivalent of three months' salary for some), and visas were withheld from three well-known Catholic intellectuals, one of whom was a close personal friend of the Pope. Nevertheless, it was generally agreed that 'they' were making prodigious efforts in order to issue visas and facilitate travel arrangements. Polish Catholics basked in the unwonted warmth of (no doubt temporary) Government approval. After all, Mr Jablonski, the Polish Head of State, and Mr Kakol were themselves going to make the journey to Rome to see this 'son of Poland' installed in the see of Peter.

\* \* \*

*Tuesday October 17th.* On the piazza outside the splendid Gothic and Baroque Cathedral on the Wawel Hill in Cracow, where forty kings and queens of Poland were crowned and buried, preparations were being made for an evening Mass of Thanksgiving. At the Cathedral's main altar Cardinal Karol Wojtyla had said Mass on September 28th, on the occasion of his twentieth anniversary as a bishop of Cracow. That was just before his departure to Rome for the fateful Conclave. And now he was no longer Cardinal of Cracow but Bishop of Rome.

People were expected in such numbers that the Cathedral itself might not be large enough to hold them. Hence the preparations in the square, where an altar had been erected and a microphone system installed, and where workmen were adding the last touches to their handiwork as twilight came on. Wishful thinking on the organisers' part, perhaps, since the authorities were playing the power game again, and had withheld permission for the event to be announced over the radio. The only publicity had been by word of mouth, and a notice written with felt pen and nailed to the door of the Curial offices and episcopal residence in the Street of the Franciscans. No matter. Everyone knew or sensed that there was to be a Mass, and it seemed as though the whole of Cracow climbed the hill towards the great Cathedral that evening. The decision to stay out of doors was more than justified. 'As the celebration reached its height,' commented Peter France, in the BBC's *Everyman* film of the event, 'there was no empty space to be seen in the whole square, and the massed heads of men and women with children on their shoulders stretched into the darkness and out into the roads leading up to the Cathedral . . . At the end of the ceremony the thousands of people began to sing spontaneously the hymn that is sung each morning in Czestochowa (the Polish national shrine to the Virgin Mary) as the Black Madonna is revealed to the faithful. God was being implored again to keep Poland free, and on this occasion, they felt, he had taken as a sacrifice the best-loved man in Poland. The people of Cracow that night offered their Cardinal Archbishop as a sacrifice to God.'

\*    \*    \*

Karol Wojtyla, firmly lodged in the Vatican, must have been only too aware of the sacrifice he had to make. It was said that on the evening before the Cardinals went into Conclave, he had asked two friends to book him on the first possible return flight to Cracow, after the Election. On the night of his election, with no possibility of making that return flight, he put a call through to his residence in Cracow. About ten of his former colleagues clustered eagerly round the telephone.

'How is it in Cracow?' he asked. 'What are you all doing?'

'We are all in tears,' came the reply.

'Then come to Rome,' the new Pope said, 'and we'll shed tears together.'

And the following morning in the Sistine Chapel, a fellow-Cardinal said to the tough old Primate of Poland, Wyszynski: 'There is sure to be great jubilation in your country today, don't you think?'

'Yes,' replied the old Cardinal, 'but there will be none in Wojtyla.'

In Cracow, after the first outburst of joy and delirium, the mood had passed into a minor key, and a desolating sense of loss had asserted itself. 'We feel a great pride, a great joy, and at the same time a great sadness, because we love him and because we know that he has gone from us,' said a woman, echoing the sentiments of many. 'We have to give him up now. He was *our* friend, but now he has gone to be the friend of the whole world. Of course we are proud to have such a man to give, but we are also sad. How could we not be?' This from a student. 'He has gone from us but he will stay in our hearts' – a woman overheard on a tram.

'Well,' said a doctor who knew Wojtyla well, 'he is a Pole. Poles who live away from Poland always yearn for their country and above all for their home town. Wojtyla will be no exception. It will be a long and sacrificial road that he must take. But no matter where he is, he will always be part of Poland.'

[1]Everyman film, *How Is It In Cracow*? BBC2, 22.10.78.
[2]Quoted in *The Times* 18.10.78.

# 2

# Be With Me On The White Mountain

BY THE FOLLOWING WEEKEND the people of Cracow had almost got used to the shock. Almost. As one admitted, 'I still don't know how to cope with it. I'm disoriented.' The strange spectacle of journalists swarming round the city, swooping on passers-by for *vox pop* comment had lost its power to amaze. Most people had grown weary of the Press and cameramen, and some were outraged by their insensitivity. Incensed by Pressmen who knocked on the door of the episcopal palace and demanded to know the nature of His Holiness's favourite foods or his taste in socks, his former housekeeper rebelled. 'He is a good and holy man, and I have nothing else to say,' she insisted as she firmly closed the door in the face of importunate seekers after sensation. Rumour had it that in the Pope's birthplace of Wadowice, the parish priest and the local schoolmaster were sitting with ice-packs on their heads trying to recover from the onslaught of the previous week.

On Saturday afternoon Cracow seemed almost deserted. Most of the journalists had left, and five hundred of its citizens had just departed in three plane loads to Warsaw on the first leg of the journey to Rome. Many of these had received personal invitations from the Pope himself – among them two hundred students whom he had instructed to be on St Peter's Square by nine on the Sunday morning, 'so that we can sing Polish songs together.'

*Sunday morning.* Even in the drizzling rain and bitter

cold, the Vatican and Polish flags manage to add trium-
phant splashes of colour to enliven the drabness. It is just
before six am and Cracow is coming to life. The flower-
sellers are already doing a brisk trade on the market square,
as people hurry, head down against the rain, to the earliest
Mass of the day. Mothers with children clutching huge
sheaves of carnations, chrysanthemums and marigolds, tied
around with yellow and white ribbon. The great twin-
towered Mariacki Church fills up, and there are so many for
Communion that when the six o'clock Mass is over it is
immediately time for the seven o'clock one to start. In place
of a homily the priest reads a pastoral letter from the
Bishops of Cracow, beseeching prayers for Jan Pawel II,
'who has left the see of Stanislaw for that of Peter', and
announcing that henceforth Mass will be said for him every
day in the Cathedral at Wawel.

Not far away is the ancient Franciscan church where
Cardinal Wojtyla used often to say Mass and make the Way
of the Cross. (In Cracow you do not ask how many churches
there are. If you do, they tell you they don't know, only the
Holy Spirit knows. At a rough count there are at least fifty.)
Like every other church in Cracow, this too is crowded and
festooned with yellow and white drapes. The to-ing and
fro-ing is ceaseless and just as we arrive, a group of young
Franciscan novices troop up to the choir, one with a moth-
eaten woolly showing beneath his habit, another clutching
an antique fur cap, and a third betraying a few centimetres
of frayed blue jeans. The time is eight am and excitement is
growing. By nine, priests are hurrying through their Mass
and the congregations are thinning out. The streets begin to
empty, and soon all of Cracow will be glued to a television
set, to see the first-ever televised Mass on the Polish net-
work. Not so long ago, Cardinal Wojtyla and the Government were locked in combat about the latter's refusal to
allow the Church sufficient access to the mass media; or to
allow a Sunday Mass to be transmitted, at least for the sake
of the sick and the aged. Now the wheel has come full circle.

It is Wojtyla's own Mass which will make the break-through.

The Pope asked for the ceremony to be held at ten rather than later in the day, so as not to keep the Italian fans from their televised football match in the afternoon. Pity the poor Polish clergy, though, condemned to say a Mass at ten a.m. on this day. Normally the churches are full at that hour, today there are perhaps fifty at the Cathedral, and even fewer elsewhere. It is the same story all over Poland. As Yves de Saint-Agnès wrote in *Paris-Match*: 'Amazing John Paul II. On the first day of his reign, he managed to empty the churches of Poland – and on a Sunday at the hour of High Mass. Strange irony of fate, to bring about what thirty-three years of a totalitarian regime, of persecution and of police harass-ment had failed to achieve.'

The apartment in Cracow where we were staying (I had come with a Polish-speaking friend from England) had eighty-eight stone steps, no lift and no television. Perhaps it was just as well. Lack of a set forced us out into the streets in search of a public one. In a café, a hotel perhaps. We stopped a scurrying nun. She was from Warsaw and didn't know her way round much better than we did, but she'd heard that there was a television set at the State-run Dom Turysty – a sort of People's Holiday Hostel which caters for coach-loads from all over Poland and the rest of the Com-munist bloc. In such a place the atmosphere was not likely to be religious. On the other hand it might be revealing. After all, we knew what the Catholic in the Cracow street felt. This might be different.

We ran all the way to the Dom Turysty, almost colliding in our haste with whole families in the same sort of hurry, on their way to friends' television sets, carrying their lunch in large paper bags. By the time we arrived at the Dom Turysty, we seemed like the last people on earth, the city outside a ghost-city. At the People's Hostel they were a bit cagey. Television set? They didn't think they had one.

Then, seeing our dismay, a passing waiter whispered that there was one on the fourth floor, if we cared to walk up. And there it was, on the landing at the top of the stairs, a large (black and white) set, protected by a glass case and securely fastened to the wall. Such chairs as were there had already been taken. It was standing room only, with a wall to lean against if you were lucky.

The ceremony in Rome had started, but our picture was faint, the commentator inaudible. Someone went to complain, and returned with a stalwart woman official carrying an enormous bunch of keys. She tried every single key in the bunch before she found one that fitted the glass housing to the set, and adjusted both the volume and the picture. It was better now, though a lift clattered and rumbled continually up and down, and an army of cleaners emerged on to our floor, rattling keys, slamming doors with vigour and dragging along huge vacuum cleaners. The cacophony was considerable, but the viewers seemed impervious to it. Apart from such noises-off, silence reigned, although as yet there was a careful absence of expression on the faces of those present.

It was time for the Cardinals to come and pay their individual homage to the new Pope, and almost the first in line was the indomitable old Polish patriot, Cardinal Wyszynski who, less than a week before, as Primate of Poland, had been Wojtyla's superior. The old man knelt to make his obeisance, ready to kiss not only the hand of the Pontiff but also his feet. Wojtyla acted swiftly to forestall him. Gently pulling the old Cardinal to his feet, he embraced him three times, in the Polish fashion, and kissed his hand. In the Dom Turysty there was a sudden explosion of coughing and sniffling and chairs were shifted this way and that, in a bid to escape the intolerable emotion aroused by the scene. The men standing near me looked at the ceiling, then inserted a finger beneath their spectacles to brush away the tears.

When the Pope wagged an admonitory finger at Cardinal

Bengsch of Berlin, the emotional pressure found a brief release in laughter. The Poles once, not very long ago, suffered much at the hands of the Germans, and though there has been a reconciliation, they are not averse to scoring the odd point over the erstwhile enemy. So they laughed when the Polish commentator (who was not very adept at names) said with a trace of chauvinism, 'This is the Polish *Pope*, and here we have a German *Cardinal*.'

For an hour, John Paul went on receiving the Cardinals. 'It was not an obeisance,' commented the Italian magazine, *Il Tempo*. 'It was an opportunity for conversation, 117 conversations.' And when the long procession of Cardinals had finally ended, John Paul began his homily. Although, in the Dom Turysty, feet were being eased out of shoes and the heat was becoming oppressive, he had their attention now. And there wasn't a man, woman or child in the place who didn't know that the new Pope wasn't only quoting Scripture when he said:

Today the new Bishop of Rome solemnly begins his ministry and the mission of Peter. In this city, in fact, Peter completed and fulfilled the mission entrusted to him by the Lord. The Lord said to him: 'When you were young you put on your own belt and walked where you liked, but when you grow old you will stretch out your hands and somebody else will put a belt around you and take you where you would rather not go.'

Peter came to Rome. What else but obedience to the mandate received from the Lord guided him and brought him to this city, the heart of the empire? Perhaps the fisherman of Galilee did not want to come here. Perhaps he would have preferred to stay there, on the shores of the lake of Genesareth, with his boat and his nets. But guided by the Lord, obedient to his mandate, he came here according to an ancient tradition (which found magnificent expression in a novel by Henryk Sienkiewicz) during Nero's persecution. Then, fearing persecution himself, he left again, but met Christ on his way out of the city. Peter spoke to him and asked, '*Quo vadis, Domine?* – where are you going, Lord?' and the Lord answered him at once, 'I am going to Rome to be crucified again.'

Although he went on to say that, in spite of being a son of Poland, he had now become a Roman, Poles all over the world understood that he was grieving.

He reminded the world that the Polish Church had always remained faithful to Rome (a fact that people in the West have often forgotten or ignored). But for the Poles, whether they were listening to him in St Peter's Square or at home in Cracow, Warsaw, Lublin, Gdansk or Poznan, the real message came at the end when he spoke to them directly in Polish. There was no longer even a pretence at holding back the tears:

To you, my dear fellow-countrymen, what shall I say? Everything that I could say fades into insignificance compared with what my heart feels and your hearts feel at this moment. So let us leave aside words. Let there remain just a great silence before God, the silence that turns into prayer. I ask you: be with me on the White Mountain and in every other place.

The reference was to *Jasna Gora*, the White Mountain, on which stood the symbol and heart-beat of the Polish nation, the monastery of Czestochowa with its famous icon of the Black Virgin. In this place, faith and patriotism find a single focus, religious history and nationhood become as one. In 1655, Charles Gustav of Sweden swept over the country with his well-trained army, and the Polish king, John Casimir, had to flee the country. It was at Czestochowa that a proud and desperate last stand was made. The enemy was strong, his numbers overpowering. But peasants, townsmen and nobles flocked to defend the sanctuary of Czestochowa. John Casimir vowed to the Virgin Mary that if peace were restored he would work to free his people from the injustices and burdens by which they were oppressed. A few days later, just before Christmas, the Swedish troops withdrew; and after that, they say, Poland awoke and found its identity as a nation. The king was able to return to his country and, in Lwow, on April 1st, 1656, in the presence of many thousands, he proclaimed the Blessed Virgin to be Queen of Poland.

So the White Mountain is a powerful symbol. The monastery of Czestochowa, it has been said, 'is the very soul of Poland'. When John Paul went on to quote from the poet Adam Mickiewicz:

> Do not cease to be with the Pope who today prays with the words of the poet: 'Holy Virgin who dost protect bright Czestochowa and dost shine in Ostrobrama,'

the listening world might well detect an innocuous, somewhat pious verse written by an obscure poet. But Mickiewicz was a hero of the previous century as well as a great poet, and Ostrobrama (the Pointed Gate) is another famous shrine of the Virgin – in Wilno, which once was part of Poland but now is in Russian-dominated Lithuania. The guarded speech which the Poles had to learn during centuries of foreign occupation has given them an uncanny knack of talking in code and reading between the lines. To quote again from *Il Tempo*: *'Chi doveva intendere, intendeve'* – the message was clearly understood by those for whom it was meant.

It was later reported in the Italian press and elsewhere that the words had been censored in Poland. The report was not true. The words were heard, the handkerchiefs came out and stayed out. The Pope then went on to speak in French, German, English, Spanish, Portuguese as well as Italian. When he added a few words in Czech, in Ukrainian, in Lithuanian and in Russian, a man standing near me burst out, 'What a diplomat! I suppose he's father to all that lot now, and we'll have to try and get used to it.'

The Polish commentator, unused to dealing with religious ceremonial, was ill-prepared by Western standards. Long patches of silence occurred, with no snatches of interesting information to fill the gaps. All the more surprising then, when, as he remarked on the enthusiasm of the multi-national crowd in St Peter's Square, he added in a burst of unexpected fervour, 'We may belong to different nations yet we are all children of the same God.' An unremarkable comment elsewhere perhaps, but on the State Television service of a People's Republic . . .

When, at the end of three and three-quarter hours of standing, shuffling, sitting and squirming, Pope John Paul announced that it was time for lunch, 'for you and also for the Pope', there was laughter and relief, and a general swooping down the stairs for lunch. One comment was significant: 'Did you notice,' said a woman to her friend, 'that when the Cardinals made their obeisance, they went away as though they had received Holy Communion?'

As we reached the restaurant, we saw three large touring coaches draw up at the kerbside. Closer inspection revealed them to be from Moscow. There was never a chance that those tourists would be exposed to the proceedings from Rome. They had been taken for a tour of the countryside, out of harm's way.

And after lunch, Cracow went off to church again to pray for the Pope. 'I appeal to every man,' he had said, '(and with what veneration the apostle of Christ must utter this word "man") – pray for me. Help me to be able to serve you.' Outside the episcopal palace in the Franciszkanska, crowds queued to pray for a while in his private chapel. In the hall three large bound books lay on a table, and in them people were inscribing affectionate messages; some were writing long tear-stained letters of farewell. They were beginning, almost without noticing it, to use the past tense when they spoke of him; it had dawned on them that he wouldn't be coming back.

That evening we called to see a woman who knew him well. She too was writing a letter to him, and she read it out to us. 'Do not worry about us,' it began, 'let *us* worry about *you*. All of us, throughout Poland, will pray for you night and day. We shall, with the help of Our Lady, serve you faithfully.' She broke down as she came to the rest of the letter. 'What you are living through, we are living through with you. It is, it must be, a holy time – no matter what the future has in store for us all. God be praised.' We left her to her tears.

'Poor Karolek,' said a girl student, using the diminutive by which he was widely known. 'I wonder how he will manage in Rome. No more ski-ing, no more mountain-climbing, no more of our Polish lakes and hills. He will miss it terribly.'[1]

[1]*Sunday Times* report by Nicholas Carroll.

# 3

# A Boy Called 'Lolek'

THE PARISH PRIEST OF Wadowice, Father Edward Zacher, proudly opened for what must have been the umpteenth time, the register of baptisms for the month of June 1920. An entry for the 20th of that month came at the bottom of a page, which was fortunate since it had overflowed its bounds. The entry recorded the baptism of one, Carolus Joseph, born to Karol Wojtyla and his wife Emilia (born Kaczorowska), on May 18th, 1920. To that original entry other inscriptions had been added in different-coloured inks:

> 1.XI.46 Priest
> 28.IX.58 Bishop
> 30.XII.63 Archbishop of Crakow
> 26.VI.67 Cardinal

right up to the final apotheosis, unique in the parish registers of Poland, and entered with a flourish just a few days before:

16.X.78 in Summum Pontificem electus, Joannes Paulus II.

In the last week, said the old priest, journalists and television teams had been eating him alive. They had come from all over the world, even from as far away as Brazil. He would be glad when they all went home and gave him some peace. Physically he was bearing up well, but mentally he was quite exhausted. Had he watched the ceremony on television? He had, of course. What was his reaction? 'I didn't cry,' he said more fiercely than was strictly necessary. 'Men don't cry. But I did have to take my glasses off several times to clean them. Don't ask me about it. You don't talk about these things, you keep them – here – in your heart.'

Wadowice is not a very large town, though its population has grown considerably since the time when the young Karol Wojtyla grew up here. Before the war it had a mere 9,000 inhabitants, but now, with creeping industrialisation, the number is nearer to 15,000. It has a paper-works and a factory which manufactures spare parts for motor-cars but it is not what anyone would call an industrial town; it is a country town for country people, a market town where peasants still bring in the local produce, the wheat, beetroot and potatoes, for sale. It is a town where everyone knows everyone else, and so it is a town that feels more like a village. Wadowice lies about fifty kilometres (about an hour's drive) from Cracow, to the south-west, at the foot of the Beskid mountains in the Western Carpathians, the range that marks the frontier with Czechoslovakia.

The Wojtylas originally came from further south, from Czanska near Kety, home of a famous fifteenth-century theologian, John of Kety. Karol senior was a junior officer in the Polish Army, an official in the Regional Draft Board based at Wadowice. A photograph in the family album taken just before young Karol was born shows a dark, good-looking man with a Kaiser-type moustache and bushy eyebrows. A stern man by all accounts, with a military passion for strict discipline. His wife, Emilia, a former school-teacher, had a small, pretty, oval face with humorous dark eyes alight with intelligence. The family was small: when Karol Jozef was born, the couple's only other child, Edward, was already fifteen.

He was born in a modest apartment on the first floor of number 7 Koscielna (Church) Street in Wadowice. The house, which has not yet become a shrine although pilgrims are now flocking there, is an ordinary apartment block on the corner of a narrow street just behind the great onion-domed church. From its windows can be seen the sun-dial on which the young Karol Wojtyla used to count the hours; and on which is written: 'Time passes, Eternity remains.' The arched entrance to the block has been decorated with flags and in one of the first floor windows, candles are burning in front of a large photograph of the new Pope, almost hidden in a riot of chrysanthemums. But for all that, it is an unremarkable, even a dingy house. Children were playing in the dusty courtyard as we went in, an ancient moped was propped up in the lobby, the peeling paint on the walls badly needed renewing, and the clatter of heels on the iron staircase produced anything but a reverent hush.

The present tenant, Zbigniew Putyra, is an old school-friend of Karol Wojtyla, who now teaches physics at the school they both went to. He moved to the apartment in 1938 when the Wojtylas moved out. Since then the apartment has been modernised. When the Wojtylas were there, all the rooms used to lead out of each other, there was no bathroom, and the lavatory could only be reached through the kitchen. But they counted themselves fortunate just the same. Unlike some families, they did have running water.

In 1927 Karol entered the 'universal' or primary school in Wadowice, where he remained until he was eleven. A school photograph dating from this time shows him to have the close-cropped, almost scalped look common to school-boys just then, but unattractive to modern eyes. The photograph was taken on a school outing to Zakopane, the nearby winter-sports resort and beauty spot in the Tatras. It was a place to which he returned again and again as he grew older.

Nothing much is known of his early years. Perhaps his parents were preoccupied with their older son Edward who after a brilliant career at high school had now qualified as a doctor and was looking forward to becoming a consultant. They were not well-off, and so Emilia took in sewing to help with the upkeep of the family.

But disaster was about to strike the Wojtyla family. On April 13th, 1929, at the age of forty-five, Emilia died giving birth to her third child, a girl who was stillborn. With Edward away working in a hospital the two Karols, father and son, were alone. Aware of his responsibilities towards a nine-year-old boy, but without the softening influence of his wife, Karol senior was a loving father but a stern disciplinarian who mapped out the boy's day with military precision. 'He was very strict,' remembers a friend. 'The programme each day was rigorous – Mass, school, a meal, an hour's free time, then homework. If Lolek was found playing in the street with friends after the prescribed time, he would be hauled back immediately.' 'Lolek' (a frequently used diminutive of Karol) made the most of his free time. Together with a friend who lived across the street, and whose parents owned a small café where he and his father used to eat their main meal, he would dash off to a nearby field to practise football.

Life was hard for the Wojtylas. The father was now trying to make ends meet on an army lieutenant's pension, and was forced to pinch and scrape. Edward, the older brother on whom so many hopes had been pinned, had died tragically, succumbing to an epidemic of scarlet fever in the hospital in which he worked. The untimely death of his son, so soon after the death of Emilia, affected the older Wojtyla deeply. Now there was only Karolek on whom to rest his hopes.

Karolek and his friends had moved to the Boys' High School (Gimnasium) in 1931. It was here, a year later, that Father Zacher first set eyes on him. 'I was sent to Wadowice in December 1932 to teach religion at the High School, and one of the first classes I took was Class Three, where the boys all sat on benches in front of me. There was one boy among them with a sad, intelligent face, and afterwards I asked the others who he was. "It's Lolek Wojtyla," they said, and they explained that he was sad because his only brother had just died.'

Father Zacher had continued to teach the boy, Lolek, for six years, and says now, 'He was the nearest thing to a genius I ever had the good fortune to teach.' The odd thing, or rather the special thing is that, despite such esteem from his masters, he was never a prig or a teacher's pet. Among his classmates, memories of him are very strong and extraordinarily affectionate. They recall that he was 'good at everything', especially languages and literature, but there is no trace of rancour or envy in the memory. He was always an independent spirit, adequately respectful to authority, but never one to curry favour. 'He was certainly one of the best pupils in the school,' remarked one portly middle-aged man in a fedora, 'and he never seemed to get bad marks in anything. But he was also one of the most loved.' 'Yes,' added his companion, 'he *was* outstandingly clever, but he didn't keep it to himself. He used to go out of his way to help other boys who were a bit slow. He never grudged his time to them.' 'Well, the fact that he was clever didn't make him stand-offish, it made him stimulating company,' said another friend. 'He was a marvellous story-teller, and conversation when he was around was always lively He had such a wide knowledge of all sorts of things. You know, he'd throw in a bit of Homer, or a line from Virgil, but there was a lot of fun and gossip there too.'

Clever as he was, there was no question of his being constantly immersed in books. Though as a very young boy he developed a life-long love of Polish literature, he was not one who could sit for long hours just reading. In fact he didn't like sitting still at all. Life held so much that was interesting and exciting. He was a sturdy, stocky boy, built for sport, and at school he was one of the best football players, proving himself a relentless and invincible goalkeeper; he liked swimming; went for long walks; loved to canoe along the Skava, and perhaps most of all he loved to ski. The Tatras, with their breathtaking beauty, were only a short distance away. They are wild and severe, and for mountaineers and skiers they present enormous difficulties; but to the boys brought up in their midst they held few terrors. From his earliest days the mountains were not only friends but part of the psychic make-up of the young Wojtyla. He loved the poems of Jan Kasprowicz which celebrated their beauty, and he knew and loved the mountain people, the Górals, whose peculiar patois he understood. All his life the Tatras have been a refuge, a place for meditation and stock-taking in times of stress.

'He came from the foothills, not the mountains,' said a doctor in Cracow who is one of Wojtyla's closest friends, 'but he *belongs* with the mountain people. He loves their songs and their poetry; he shares their simplicity, their sense of humour, their independence, their love of freedom. The mountain people were never serfs, so they symbolise the equality that exists between man and man; they have always been in love with freedom. Karol Wojtyla has a lot of the mountain man in his make-up. He too is in love with freedom.'

The young Wojtyla seems to have left an indelible impression on the mind of his schoolfellows, one which has not yet been overlaid by the patina of special veneration owed to a Pope. Perhaps most of all they are proud of his skill as an actor. 'He wasn't just good, he was very, very good,' they say, and they recall the time when a visiting director told him, 'One day you will become a great actor.' There was no school production in which he didn't take part, and it was usually the leading part. When the school drama group toured south-east Poland with a repertoire ranging from modern Polish drama to Shakespeare, he produced many of the plays himself. He was renowned not only for his acting but for his superb dancing, performing Strauss waltzes, folk dances and the difficult Polish mazurkas, polonaises and Krakowiaks with equal abandon and skill.

Almost the last thing mentioned by Wojtyla's former schoolmates is his piety; which at least underlines that it was not excessive and did not stand in the way of his other activities. But his father, a deeply religious man, had passed on his own strong faith to his son. Karol served on the altar at Mass each morning and ran a religious society at school. Yet his literary, dramatic and athletic interests are more remembered. An incident which occurred towards the end of his school career is significant. Just before he was about to sit for his school-leaving exams (Matura), the school received an official visit from the man who, more than any other, was to shape the course of Wojtyla's life – Bishop (later Cardinal) Adam Stefan Sapieha, Metropolitan of Cracow. Wojtyla, probably because of his fine voice, was chosen to propose a vote of thanks on behalf of the pupils. 'He did it,' remembers one of them, 'better than any of the masters could have done.'

Sapieha was visibly impressed and turned to Father Zacher who was sitting by his side. 'Is that boy going to be a priest?' he asked.

Zacher had long ago wondered the same thing, but had been at pains not to suggest it. So he shook his head. 'Doesn't look like it at the moment,' he replied.

'Pity,' said the bishop, 'he'd make a good one.'

Sapieha went back to Cracow, but he had not seen the last of Karol Wojtyla.

\*     \*     \*

When the news broke on October 16th, 1978, Wadowice was stunned and disbelieving. 'I didn't know whether I was drunk or dreaming,' said one. Most people refused to believe the evidence of their ears, until they saw it confirmed on a television news programme. Then they rushed out into the streets and into each other's apartments, 'kissing each other and weeping for joy'.

The friend with whom the young Wojtyla used to go for

walks and practise football was in the kitchen of his home in Koscielna Street. His wife was watching television in an adjoining room. He heard the words HABEMUS PAPAM, but could not hear the words that followed. Suddenly there was a shriek, and he rushed into the other room to see what had happened. He found his wife in a state of collapse. 'Jesus, Maria,' she sobbed, 'do you know what they've done? They've made Lolek Pope!'

\*        \*        \*

In the summer of 1938 the two Karols moved away from Wadowice for good – and went to Cracow, 50 kms away, one of the world's most beautiful cities. Without Cracow, it has been said, there would be no Poland. Certainly it is difficult to know how the guidebooks would stay in business without it. It is the Royal town, the cultural centre of Poland, one of the priceless jewels of Europe. Royal City, Holy City, the Polish Athens are but some of the titles bestowed on it down the ages; it is a treasure house of art and architecture almost unrivalled in Europe. Sited above a curve of the Vistula river, it is dominated by the limestone hill of Wawel which was once fortified to defend the crossing of that river from the countless enemies which threatened it. The fortified castle became the Royal Castle, home of Poland's kings and the historical shrine of the whole nation; while the adjoining Cathedral became its religious centre. (It is richly symbolic that in this ancient capital Castle and Cathedral should be so close together, forming, as it were, two halves of the same whole.) Cracow enters the history books in the ninth century as a leading European commercial centre, and by the middle of the twelfth century had become the capital of Poland, as it remained until in 1609, by decree of King Sigismund III, it was supplanted by Warsaw. Its importance in the Middle Ages made it a target for invading bands of Tartars who in 1241 succeeded at last in capturing the city, razing it to the ground and massacring all its inhabitants. (The only time in Cracow's history that it was destroyed.) Within two decades it had risen phoenix-like from its own ashes, and by the middle of the fourteenth century was more prosperous and more beautiful than ever.

As a centre of learning it was almost unique in medieval times, its University – the Jagiellonian – being the oldest in Central Europe after that of Prague, which was a mere sixteen years older. The Jagiellonian (usually referred to as the UJ, which is pronounced Oo-yot) was founded in 1364 by King Casimir the Great. After his death it declined for a brief spell, but recovered when his daughter, Jadwiga, – Poland's 'sainted queen' who had married the Grand Duke of Lithuania, Wladyslaw Jagiello, and united the two countries – bequeathed all her jewels to pay for its restoration. By the middle of the fifteenth century it was famous far beyond the borders of Poland for its achievements in law and its openness to new ideas in science and philosophy; men came from all over Europe to study there, Germans, Czechs, Hungarians, Swiss and others besides. Eventually the UJ became the European centre for astronomy, mathematics and geography, perhaps its most famous student being the astronomer Mikolaj Kopernik (Copernicus 1473–1543). It was here in Cracow that Copernicus came to doubt that the earth was at the centre of the universe, and, moving away from that geocentric principle which had hitherto never been questioned, wrote De Revolutionibus Orbium Caelestium, which created an entirely new picture of the universe, in which the earth and other planets orbited round the sun. It was a revolutionary theory which had an immense influence on the future course of European science.

Nor was Copernicus the Jagiellonian's only famous son. Others were Dr Johann Faustus, magician and astrologer, the original of Goethe's Faust; and, man of a different genre, Vladimir Ilyich Lenin who, though not precisely a student at the University, in the years 1912–1914 came regularly to read and study in its elegant and well-stocked library.

And now there is another, whose renown will at least equal theirs – the first Polish Pope in history – Karol Jozef Wojtyla. Wojtyla entered the Jagiellonian University in 1938 to study Polish language and literature (Polish studies) and philosophy. His old teacher from the Wadowice Gimnasium, Father Zacher, admits to being surprised at his choice of course. Perhaps he had gone on hoping that Wojtyla might enter the University's excellent theological department which had been founded in 1400.

The young man was immediately popular with his fellow-students and was generally regarded as good company, immensely friendly, a man who loved a joke. His study of Polish literature gave him ample excuse for indulging his love for the stage, which he now fully intended to make his career. He joined the celebrated *Studio Dramatyczne 1939*, the student group which experimented with verse dramas based on heroic themes from Polish history; modern plays; reviews; as well as providing a forum for public speaking. It was a kind of theatre workshop which explored new frontiers in drama.

In his spare time Wojtyla began to study seriously for a diploma in Drama. A woman who belonged to the same drama group and was a close friend, remembers that they performed a play by Marian Niżynski, *Knight of the Moon*, based on an old Cracovian legend. The actors each represented a different sign of the Zodiac, and Wojtyla being large and muscular was Taurus. When the play was over he was liable to take off his bull's head, shout, 'Look out, I'm a wild bull,' and chase the others round the stage. The play was immensely successful and the students' performance can often be seen referred to in books written about the (very lively) Cracow theatre. (Today the city has eight theatres.) Photographs on old programmes and posters reveal that Wojtyla had become a strikingly handsome nineteen-year-old.

'Everyone was quite sure he would be an actor,' said a fellow-student. 'He was exceptionally good. Part of the secret was that voice of his. It was powerful and hauntingly beautiful.'

These were halcyon days, untroubled, it seems, by forebodings, although jackboots were on the march across Europe. Czechoslovakia had been betrayed and had fallen, Austria had suffered its *Anschluss*, and from Berlin, Hitler, having prepared the ground carefully, was making minatory noises over the Polish Corridor. And over in the East the Russians waited.

All that must have seemed a million miles away as Karol Wojtyla and his friends at the UJ, so soon to be engulfed by the whirlpool, pursued their social life and their studies. Wojtyla had begun to write poetry, and he and his friends (usually the ones from the drama group) formed a circle of young student poets, holding literary evenings during which they read out their own poems and those of their favourite poets. Wojtyla's own favourite, Emil Zegadlowicz, came from Wadowice. Like himself, Zegadlowicz was a countryman, and his poems had a strongly bucolic flavour, full of nostalgia for the sights and sounds of rural Poland. Wojtyla's own poetry, then as later, owed much to him.

There were no doubts left in his mind: he would become an actor and a great one. Friends in the group, of whom one was Mieczyslaw Kotlarczyk, well-known in the Polish theatre today, encouraged him to go ahead. The future was bright.

But it was less bright than they thought. It was already the summer of 1939, and Armageddon was at hand.

# 4

# Underground

ALTHOUGH SHE IS almost always referred to as East European, Poland is at the centre of Europe. Somewhere in a Warsaw park there is a stone which, they assure you, marks the exact geometrical centre of the Continent. That may or may not be accurate, but what is beyond dispute is that Poland lies at a crossroads of Europe – an uncomfortable fact of geography which has caused her much suffering throughout history, laying her open to attack from all points of the compass. From the east have come unending waves of Mongolians, Lithuanians and Russians; from the west, Huns, Teutons, Prussians and Volkdeutsch; from the south, Tartars, Turks, Magyars and Austrians; and from the north, in their turn, came the armies of Sweden. Poland is the eternal prey, eternally exposed to the chill winds of history, her rich granaries and mines coveted by greedy neighbours. As Igor Stravinsky once trenchantly put it: 'If you pitch your tent in the middle of Fifth Avenue, you are likely to be hit by a bus.'

In the eighteenth century she disappeared altogether during the Partitions, when her Prussian, Russian and Austrian conquerors decided to carve her up and share out the pieces. The history books call it the *Finis Poloniae*, the end of Poland, and it must have seemed very like the end: the misery of the three Partitions, during which the Polish people were reduced to the status of serfs and even the use of their language was, at times and in certain places, forbidden, lasted from 1772 until 1918. Poland did not reappear on the world maps until the end of the First World War; and even then, after 1918, she had to fight to establish all her frontiers. The most intensive fighting was in 1920 against the Bolsheviks, who actually reached the gates of Warsaw and of Lwow. 'Those who could fight did so; those who couldn't prayed.'

On August 15th, the Feast of the Assumption of the Blessed Virgin, the avalanche of the Red Army was halted and massively defeated. It was a tremendous victory for the Poles, attributed by some to the genius of Marshal Pilsudski and by others to the intervention of the Blessed Virgin. (Today most Poles would share the credit between them!) This experience was a cathartic one and henceforth a fear of Communism took deep root in the Polish sub-conscious.

The Poles never gave invaders an easy time of it. Being so often oppressed, they developed a stubbornness and skill in the face of oppression which made it easy for them to follow the advice Jean-Jacques Rousseau had given them on the brink of the Partitions: 'You cannot prevent them swallowing you,' he said, 'but at least make sure you give them indigestion.'

*     *     *

After many years of mutual abuse, on August 22nd, 1939, Germany and the Soviet Union concluded a treaty of friendship, which took the whole world by surprise. The writing on the wall was clear: with the help (or guaranteed non-interference) of his new ally, Hitler had *carte blanche* to do what he wanted with Europe. He intended to make full use of the opportunity to impose a New Order and to establish the beginnings of the Thousand Year Reich.

At dawn on September 1st, 1939, Hitler attacked Poland. From north, west and south, German armies poured over Polish soil, while death and destruction rained from the skies. Two days later World War II had begun.

'We were ready to defend our country with our bare fists,' says a former Polish soldier. 'All the old divisions in society disappeared. Everyone was prepared to die, not for his house, not for his property, but for his country. But the mechanised power of the Germans was too much for us. It was a case of machines against people, horses against tanks, lances against cannon.'

The campaign in Poland was brief and bloody. Incredibly brave as they were, without help from outside the Poles did not stand a chance. Within forty-eight hours their air force was destroyed; within a week most of their army was routed, and one week later its straggling remnants were pinned down and decimated. On September 6th Cracow fell, and on the afternoon of September 8th German troops reached Warsaw. (In the course of the war, many European cities were bombed, but what was done to Warsaw defied description.)

On September 17th the Russians moved in to help dismember the corpse. On the pretext that Poland no longer existed and that therefore the Polish-Soviet non-aggression pact was null and void, the Red Army proceeded to trample on an already prostrate Poland and to do a deal with Germany whereby Poland and most lands to the east were divided between them. It was the Fourth Partition of Poland and by far the most savage. Hitler was keeping one promise amid a host of broken ones: 'I shall make Poland,' he had sworn, 'a long-forgotten name on ancient maps.'

Many thousands of prisoners-of-war were taken by both sides. The ordinary soldiers were later allowed home; the officers were taken to POW camps. Those in Germany survived and were released after the war, whilst those in the Soviet Union perished in Katyn Wood, each with a hole in his head. Nobody, either German or Russian, has ever admitted to the crime, which remains one of the great unsolved crimes of history. Each accuses the other. But the tiny saplings which grow on the graves of the murdered men give signs of being planted in 1940 when the area was still in Soviet hands.

What was left of Poland, after the Russians had seized their share to the east and the Germans had formally annexed their former provinces (and a few more besides) in the west, was designated the General Government, a sort of overspill area providing cheap labour and extra food for the Germans. Hans Frank, a leading Nazi, was made Governor General. 'The Poles,' he declared, the day after he took office, 'shall be the slaves of the German Reich.'

Poles, like Jews, were *Untermenschen*, sub-humans, and were to be exterminated like vermin. As far as Hitler was concerned they had no right to life, but he intended to use some of them – the Slavs not the Jews – as a workforce, educated only to the barest minimum at which they could read their masters' instructions and count up to one hundred.

By October 2nd, Hitler had outlined his plans for Poland to Hans Frank and other officials.

> The Poles are especially born for low labour . . . There can be no question of improvement for them. It is necessary to keep the standard of life low in Poland and it must not be permitted to rise . . . the Government General should be used by us merely as a source of unskilled labour . . . every year the labourers needed by the Reich could be procured from there . . .
>
> (The priests) will preach what we want them to preach. If any priest acts differently, we shall make short work of him; the task of a priest is to keep the Poles quiet, stupid and dull-witted.[1]

With such a policy in mind, it was logical that every educated person must be regarded as an enemy and marked down for destruction.

There should be one master only for the Poles, the

Germans. Two masters, side by side, cannot and must not exist. Therefore, all representatives of the Polish intelligentsia are to be exterminated.

The policy of wiping out the Polish Jews, intelligentsia, nobility and clergy was known to the Germans by the tidy name of 'House-cleaning.' Himmler and Heydrich were assigned to the cleaning out of the Jews; Hans Frank had a double task – the plunder of what was left of Poland to provide food and supplies and forced labour for the Reich; and the elimination of the intelligentsia. There was a code-name for the latter operation, good, clean, military action that it was: the *Ausserordentliche Befriedigungsaktion* (AB Aktion) – Extraordinary Pacification Action. It took considerable time to get it organised, and Hans Frank was nothing if not methodical. (He recorded everything in forty-two volumes of his diary which were presented in evidence at the Nuremberg Trials.) It was not until May 1940 that he began to achieve results.

On May 30th, Frank noted in his diary that he had made progress. That day he had spurred on his police aides by telling them of 'some thousands' of intellectuals taken or about to be taken; and had asked for their full co-operation. It was, he told them, a direct command from Hitler, who had expressed himself as follows:

> The men capable of leadership in Poland must be liquidated. Those following them . . . must be eliminated in their turn. There is no need to burden the Reich with this . . . no need to send these elements to Reich concentration camps.

These 'elements' could be dealt with on the spot. The chief of the Security Police (Gestapo) was able to report to the meeting that 2,000 men and several hundred women had already been apprehended. Most of them had been eliminated. A second batch of intellectuals was now being rounded up for 'summary sentence' – a polite euphemism for liquidation.

The words 'Final Solution' had already entered the German vocabulary, and it was not long before Frank was announcing to his henchmen: 'As far as the Jews are concerned, I want to tell you quite frankly that they must be done away with in one way or another . . . Gentlemen, I must ask you to rid yourselves of all feeling of pity. We must annihilate the Jews.'[2]

Already in February 1940, Oberführer Richard Glücks, head of the Concentration Camps Inspectorate had discovered a 'suitable site' for a new 'quarantine camp' at Auschwitz, a desolate, unhealthy, marshy place, a few miles away from Cracow, where Governor General Hans Frank had set up his headquarters.

\*       \*       \*

The Governor General had taken up his abode in the historic Wawel Castle, once the residence of kings. (It has, in fact, been the peculiar destiny of Cracow that its conquerors have preferred to live in it rather than reduce it to ashes.)

From here then, the work of terror was directed. Within a few days of their arrival in Cracow, the Germans had closed the Jagiellonian University. On November 6th the teaching staff were invited to a meeting, and, believing that this concerned plans for re-opening, they almost all walked into the trap. (One professor, meeting a friend en route, was persuaded, over a cup of tea in a café, not to attend. Emerging from the café, the two horrified men 'saw the professors being loaded on to trucks by the Gestapo.') Unlike the massacre of professors in Lwow in 1941 there were no summary executions, but 200 academics were taken to concentration camps, (mainly to Sachsenhausen.) Seventeen of them died in the camps or soon after their eventual release.

The students were no less endangered. To be recognised as such meant death or deportation – either to a concentration camp or to forced labour in Germany. Many of Karol Wojtyla's friends of both sexes had already been arrested by the Gestapo and had simply disappeared (some for ever, others to emerge from camps like Auschwitz when the war was over). It was obvious that the only way to stay alive was to merge with the rest of the population and become a labourer. The Germans were issuing *Arbeitskarten* (work cards) and anyone caught without one invited instant deportation to forced labour.

In 1940 Wojtyla went to hew stones in a quarry belonging to the Solvay chemical works at Zakrzow outside Cracow. But he did not stop being a student. The Poles were not to be brow-beaten, and the University had simply gone underground, adopting the 'flying university' tactics developed by Polish patriots during the partitions of the nineteenth century. In those oppressive times the clergy watched over the Polish language, teaching it together with the catechism. All over Cracow (as in the other University towns) students resisted the wilful destruction of their culture, meeting in private houses, apartments, cellars, church-crypts and the backs of shops to continue their studies and plan other ways of resisting the oppressor. And as the voice of protest has always found powerful expression in plays and poetry, they set up an underground theatre. It was in the room that Karol Wojtyla rented from his friend Mieczyslaw Kotlarczyk (also from Wadowice) at number 10 Tyniecka Street in Debniki that the celebrated *Teatr Rapsodyczny* was born. In this room Kotlarczyk, Wojtyla and others would recite Polish poetry and perform verse dramas before secret audiences of fifteen to twenty. The plays they performed were patriotic dramas which sounded the note of freedom and stiffened the morale of those who watched them. One of their most popular performances was 'Wyspianski's Hour' – carefully chosen extracts from the plays of the great 19th Century playwright, painter and poet who used historical themes to illuminate the sufferings of the time. It is not difficult to understand his popularity in the dark days of 1940.

But *Teatr Rapsodyczny* was just one of many weapons of the Resistance movement, and most of those who took part in it were involved in other clandestine activities too. The theatre remained undiscovered, but many of its young members were caught and dealt with in other contexts. The whole of Poland was a hotbed of resistance, and Karol Wojtyla did his share. Those who knew him at this period remember both his courage and his qualities of leadership. He was someone to rely on in difficult situations, since he remained calm when faced with an emergency, and could almost always come up with an intelligent and workable solution. His bravery was beyond dispute. A schoolfriend, Jerzy Zubrzycki, who is now a professor of sociology in Australia, told *Time* magazine: 'He lived in danger daily of losing his life. He would move about the occupied cities taking Jewish families out of the ghettos, finding them new identities and hiding places. He saved many families threatened with execution.'

Powerful forces were at work in the young Wojtyla. All around him he saw suffering and misery; men and women famished and reduced to the level of chattels; children snatched from their parents and deported; Jewish families brutally rounded up and sent God knew where; schools and universities closed down; and underneath the dogged determination and courage of the Poles, the constant fear: fear for one's family and friends, fear for oneself; fear of the knock on the door in the middle of the night; of sudden arrest by the Gestapo. Nazi jackboots strutting around the city underlined the atmosphere of terror. The brutality he witnessed every day, the degrading conditions in which he and his fellow-labourers toiled, affected him with something close to despair. His misery was compounded by his father's death in the first year of the war. Father and son had become very close since their arrival in Cracow, the relationship between them being one of deep and devoted friendship. When his father died the young Wojtyla was bitterly conscious of being alone in the world, with death and wretchedness all around him.

And yet those months in the stone-quarry may have opened his eyes to truths he had not seen before, and perhaps set his course for the future. Years afterwards when he had become a priest, he wrote an extraordinarily powerful poem about those days, a difficult, sometimes obscure poem, but in many ways the finest he ever wrote. 'The Stone-quarry' contains all the themes which would come to characterise his ministry: the immense compassion, the sensitivity to human dignity, the respect for manual labour, the longing to serve, the awareness of love as the driving force of life, and the perception of a Reality that transcends the observable world. In it he spoke of the anger and pain implicit in the work of quarrying stone: the cracked and blistered hands 'satured with hardship', the tired eyes, heaving torsos and knotted muscles, the boots ankle-deep in mud. (One day a work-mate had died, his temples split open 'like plaster cracking on a wall.') But he finds grandeur as well as pain: it is not the power-drill which shatters the stone, but the worker who holds it in his hand. In the violent landscape of stone he seems to see the human soul creating itself, the visible reality reflecting the interior heart: man gains strength from the stone; sureness of hand and eye teach balance and lead to maturity. When blasting was in progress a massive charge was laid to the age-old stone, and in the fury of the charge – which shattered the stone into a million fragments – he recognised an explosion of energy which he could only compare to love, Wojtyla is overwhelmed with pity for his fellow-workers, particularly the young 'who are searching for a way'. He wanted to teach them not to be afraid: 'Oh, see how one can love in such deep anger.'

From being a stone-hewer he had been promoted to assistant shot-firer, responsible for placing the cartridges and fuses ready for dynamiting the rock. He disliked the work at Solvay, but had become very attached to his fellow-workers, rapidly becoming a leader among them, not hesitating to speak out in an attempt to improve the conditions in which they had to work. He improvised a recreation and education centre in the factory, organised lectures and encouraged the workers to read. At all costs the Germans must be prevented from turning them into a mass of uneducated serfs. The workers were only too eager to accept whatever he could provide for them. In fact they frequently offered to do his own work for him so that he could go off and study – an offer he never accepted.

The crisis in his own life was coming to a head. One day when he was crossing the street from his apartment block in the Tyniecka, he was knocked down by a tram and fractured his skull. For a time his life hung by a thread, and as he lay delirious he felt a sudden strong call to the priesthood. Ill and weak as he was, he struggled against the idea, fending it off. It was not that he had never considered the idea of becoming a priest, but his sights were firmly set on the theatre. Once again he hardened his resolve. Determination to escape this fate may have prompted his unusually rapid recovery, to the point where the doctors remarked not only a complete cure but an amazing improvement in his powers of memory as a result of the trauma he had undergone.

But scarcely a few months later he met with a second equally serious accident, in which he narrowly escaped being crushed to death by a truck. (Ever since that time he has had one shoulder higher than the other, a fact which has given him a permanent stoop.) In a hospital bed again and defenceless, he felt the summons to the priesthood more insistently; and this time he could not escape so lightly. He knew that he had reached a watershed in his life, and that a decision must be made without delay.

Perhaps he was helped to a decision by his friend Jan Tyranowski, a tailor by trade and more than twice Wojtyla's age. Tyranowski, who belonged to the same parish as himself, had a decisive influence on the younger man's thought and growing spirituality. A true lay apostle, he had gathered round him a discussion group of five young men, among them Wojtyla, to whom he recommended the study of St John of the Cross. This sixteenth-century Spanish mystic and poet had written of the *via negativa*, the darkness in which the soul finds God after it has first rid itself of all delight in the senses. The concept was a difficult one, but it is easy to understand its appeal for those who were living through the impenetrable darkness of the Occupation. Wojtyla came to share Tyranowski's enthusiasm for John of the Cross, and through it to reflect more deeply on his own search for Divine truth. He never forgot the debt he owed to his master, referring to him years later, after his death in 1947, as 'a true apostle of God's greatness.'

Whatever the reasons, Wojtyla now accepted that he must become a priest. His vocation had been born of the chaos and savagery of the Occupation, which had driven him to put his life at the service of others, to keep the flickering flame of humanity alive in such profound darkness.

Like the University and like the high schools, the official seminaries in Poland had all been closed down, the seminarians deported or killed. So the seminaries too had gone underground, and continued to accept new students in spite of the proscription. In 1942 Karol Wojtyla joined the illegal theological department of the Jagiellonian University – at risk of his life. He continued to work at Solvay and with his other resistance work. It seems probable that he was involved (as he *certainly* was later) with the Bratnia Pomoc Studentow, a secret organisation through which students helped each other to find food, money and shelter.

Wojtyla's life followed this precarious pattern from 1942 until August 1944 when he quite suddenly disappeared from view. Various romantic explanations have been put forward to account for his disappearance, and the most romantic of these suggested that he had married, that his wife had been murdered by the Gestapo and that, broken-hearted, he had then decided to become a celibate priest.

The truth is simpler, less romantic but almost equally dramatic. One of the methods the Germans regularly used to terrorise the Poles was the *łapanka*, the practice of making a sudden swoop on a street, any street, cordoning it off, setting up road-blocks, and arresting or shooting all those who had the misfortune to be there at the time. When Warsaw rose in revolt in August 1944, the Germans stepped up this practice throughout the rest of Poland, as a means of discouraging them from following suit. After a particularly vicious *łapanka* that August, in which young Wojtyla narrowly escaped being caught, his superior, Archbishop Adam Stefan Sapieha decided to act. Fearing for the lives of his handful of students, he decided to take them under his own wing and keep them hidden in his residence in Franciszkanska Street. Once there, they had no option but to stay there, since they were now without work papers. In any case, Karol Wojtyla was now on the Germans' list of wanted men, and they were actively searching for him.

Archbishop Sapieha was a remarkable man. At the beginning of the war, the Primate (Cardinal Hlond) had, at the insistence of the Polish Government, reluctantly gone to France, but Sapieha, the next most senior prelate, had stayed and had stood up to the Germans. The people of Cracow loved him, and the Germans, however profoundly disapproving of Polish aristocrats and clerics (he was a prince by birth), respected Sapieha, who was palpably unafraid of them.

Although Sapieha must have been marked down for eventual elimination, perhaps Hans Frank deemed it more prudent to delay the execution. The Governor General would occasionally pay the old man a visit, and when he did so, his reluctant host would pointedly serve him the vile black bread, beetroot conserve and coffee made from grain, which were all the hungry Poles were given to eat.

The last time that he called on the Cardinal he did not suspect that, hidden in the building, were five young seminarians, one of whom was the wanted Wojtyla.

But the long agony of the German Occupation was almost over; and on January 12th, 1945 the Russian 'liberators' swept through Poland in a tidal wave. For the moment they were welcome. In six years the Germans had killed six million, three hundred thousand Poles, three million of whom were Jews. To put it perhaps more starkly, about one quarter of the entire population had been killed.

\*     \*     \*

'Life is strange,' mused the old priest in Wadowice. 'They tried to wipe Poland off the face of the earth. Yet now Hitler is dead, the Nazis are no more, and the despised Poland has given a Pope to the world.'

1. *The Rise and Fall of the Third Reich,* Shirer, William L., Pan Books. Chapter 27, memorandum from Martin Bormann produced at Nuremberg.
2. Adapted from op. cit.

# 5

# 'Liberation'

Now that the war and the German Occupation were over, Karol Wojtyla was free to come out of hiding and continue his theological studies openly at the University. Yet the freedom left a lot to be desired; it was not exactly the Liberation for which he and many of his compatriots had hoped. 'We did not foresee an end like this,' says the colonel in George Andrzejewski's brilliant novel, *Ashes and Diamonds*. 'We thought that not only would Germany come out of the war defeated, but Russia too. Things have turned out rather differently.' Andrzejewski's novel catches the despair of people trapped between two tyrannies, as the Germans move out, the Communists move in and anarchy takes over. 'I don't know what this new Poland is like,' says the lawyer Kossecki to Podgorsky who is a Communist:

'What it's like?' Podgorski repeated. 'How can I put it in a few words? It's difficult, that's probably the best way to describe the tangle of conflicts and contrasts which we're faced with at every step and which we certainly shan't solve tomorrow or the day after. Anyway you'll soon find out how things are here. The war's coming to an end, but the fight here is only just beginning. And it won't be a fight for just a year or even two ... You might ask me, for instance, whether our Party has support from what is known as the broad masses of the Polish people?

And the answer is that we haven't yet. . . . Some people hate us openly, others in secret, while still others simply don't trust us, don't know us, don't realise what the fight is about or why the revolution here must take this course instead of another . . . Unfortunately many people don't understand, or don't want to. Hence the bitterness, disappointment, complaints, exhaustion, thousands of young people led astray, thousands of pitiful *émigrés* . . .'[1]

There had been two main Resistance groups during the Occupation, the Home Army (AK), much the larger, receiving its instructions from the Polish Government-in-Exile in London, the other smaller group, the People's Army (AL) (which did not start its activities until after Hitler had attacked the Soviet Union) receiving theirs from Moscow. Long before the end of the war the latter group was preparing its ground; and on July 22nd, 1944 a Committee of National Liberation was set up in Lublin – on the first strip of liberated Poland. This Committee proclaimed a new Social Order based on an alliance with the Soviet Union. Few people in Poland could accept it; for five years they had fought for their independence and now it was being stolen from them. They attempted to assert this independence in the Warsaw Uprising, but in vain. Soviet policy did not allow any help to reach them, and the Poles were doomed to defeat. In January 1945 Poland found itself with a Government of National Unity, with Wladyslaw Gomulka – one of the leaders in the AL Resistance group – as Vice-Premier and Secretary-General of the Workers' Party, and Boleslaw Bierut – brought in from Moscow – as President of the Republic.

Naturally enough, the London-based Government under Mikolajczyk refused to recognise the Lublin administration, backed as it was by the Soviet Union; and the most tragic and bitter fighting broke out, this time between Pole and Pole. For two years, while Poland struggled to rebuild its shattered cities – in the case of Warsaw this meant quite literally building over a vast graveyard – the fighting continued. The Home Army Resistance groups dispersed in order to escape being taken to camps in the Soviet Union, and then reassembled in order to set free their friends who were being captured and tortured in prisons throughout the country.

In 1947 a 'free' election was held. Candidates of parties other than the Communist one were beaten up or shot, canvassers were imprisoned, and all their literature was impounded. Not surprisingly the Soviet-supported parties won by an overwhelming majority in every district. To many Poles this was the true *Finis Poloniae*, and, tragically, the destruction was being achieved not by foreign hordes but by Poles themselves.

It was in this highly-charged atmosphere that Wojtyla continued his training as a priest, and it was not long before he came near to losing his new freedom. In 1945 he narrowly escaped arrest by the Russians when he and a group of fellow-students gathered in the market place of Cracow and defiantly sang patriotic songs, which in Poland always express a yearning for freedom. They managed to disperse in time, but it was a close call.

Russian troops were still on Polish soil, and one day Wojtyla had a strange encounter with one of them. He was taking his turn as porter at the seminary where he lived, when the door-bell rang. On the step was a young Russian soldier. 'What do you want?' asked Wojtyla cautiously. 'I want to enter the seminary,' came the reply. The seminarian was speechless; the statement from such a person at such a time was astonishing and unbelievable. But he was curious and didn't want to let the soldier go. He invited him in and they talked for a long time.

'He did not enter the seminary,' recalls Wojtyla, 'but I personally learned a great truth from our encounter: that God can penetrate the minds of men in the most unpromising situations, and in spite of systems and regimes which deny His existence. This young man had scarcely ever been inside a church. At school and later at work he had been continually assured, "There is no God." And in spite of everything he kept on saying: "But I always knew that God *did* exist . . . and now I should like to learn something about Him . . ." [2] The incident made a deep impression on Wojtyla, and he has never lost sight of its significance, that man is never without God if he wants to find him.

He was deeply involved now in the students' self-help organisation which had been started during the Occupation and which was now very efficiently organised. As everybody in Poland had his own troubles, no one was prepared or able to help the students, so they had to look after themselves and each other, finding food, books, clothing and accommodation on their own initiative. The Council of the organisation was made up of representatives of all the various departments within the University, and Karol Wojtyla represented the theological department. He was vice-chairman. If the students had been able to have their way he would have been chairman but the regime would not allow a clerical student to be in charge. The students' self-help organisation was a genuine co-operative, and it worked because it had to and because everyone concerned wanted it to. Wojtyla seemed to everyone the ideal person to have at the helm. He was 'extraordinarily wise', says a former fellow-student. 'I can't say that any of us would have forecast his becoming Pope, and yet we recognised that somehow he was bigger than anybody else. Not just that he was bigger physically, but a bigger person in every way. He was no older than the rest of us, yet everyone had complete trust in his wisdom – to such an extent that when he wasn't around we used to make decisions on the basis of "What would Wojtyla do in this situation?" Even then he was a tremendously impressive – and tremendously human – person.'

His great friend of those days was a medical student. They had met during the Occupation after the young man's brother had been shot by the Gestapo. Wojtyla, hearing the news, had gone to see him, and the two had become firm friends. 'It was the worst period of my life, but he taught me to come to terms with it,' says the friend, today an eminent surgeon. They had worked together on the students' Council. 'The meetings used to go on till the early hours of the morning,' Dr M. recalls, 'and then I'd walk him back to the seminary, and we'd still be talking an hour later. He was always brimming with ideas.'

But his student days in Cracow were drawing to a close. On November 1st, 1946, Karol Jozef Wojtyla was ordained priest by Archbishop Sapieha. He was twenty-six years of age. Next morning, on All Souls' Day, one of the great feasts of the Polish liturgical year, he said his first Mass in the crypt of St Leonard in Wawel Cathedral.

It was a bad time to be entering the priesthood, though it was not yet as bad as it would later become. The attitude of the Provisional Government towards the Catholic Church was still cautious. Most Poles (even many Communists) were devout Catholics with a thousand-year tradition of identifying their faith with their Polishness and with their independence as a nation. Apart from that crucial fact – and nobody can even begin to understand Poland without appreciating this inter-penetration of faith and patriotism – the Church stood high in the estimation of the Polish people. During the 150 years of the Partitions, it had epitomised the nation's hopes; prayer was the only expression of patriotism that the conquerors could not suppress. It had openly challenged the extreme right-wing tendencies of the pre-war Government, and the overt left-wing activity of the Opposition. In the struggle against the Nazis it had led the way; the Poles would not easily forget that three thousand of their priests had been killed or had lost their lives in concentration camps during the Occupation (the estimates vary); nor that almost one thousand of their churches had been destroyed by enemy action.

So for the first two years the Government trod warily,

fearful of catching a crab, and being in any case forced to concentrate on consolidating their own power and on the enormous tasks of reconstruction which faced them. They regarded the Church as an irrelevant anachronism, an unwanted legacy from the past. In time they hoped to dispose of it, but just then a showdown would have been inconvenient.

Nevertheless, right from the start there were open acts of hostility. They suspended the Concordat with the Vatican, for example, in 1945. To some extent the Vatican's own obduracy was responsible: Pope Pius XII was usually thought to be a Germanophile and he was certainly an unswerving anti-Communist. The agreement between Roosevelt, Churchill and Stalin at Yalta had confirmed Russia's hold on Poland's eastern territories (about two-fifths of the entire country), and the Potsdam Agreement in 1945 had compensated Poland for the loss by restoring (after 600 years in German hands) her ancient Slav territories on the Oder and Neisse rivers, thus shifting her westward and giving her an entirely new set of frontiers; and at the same time making her, for the foreseeable future, a prime target for the German revanchists who resented the loss of their territories.

The whole issue, as may be imagined, was a very sensitive one for both Poles and Germans. The Vatican would not recognise the post-war frontiers until a peace treaty was concluded, and until that time refused to appoint diocesan bishops to the territory still claimed by Germany. Pius XII gave the Primate of Poland, Cardinal Hlond, authority to organise the Church in these territories and he appointed five Apostolic Administrators (i.e. not full bishops) under the jurisdiction of neighbouring bishops. Further than that he could not go.

Whatever the Vatican's attitude had been it is probable that the Soviet-dominated Government would still have revoked the Concordat, as indeed it had been revoked in every country under Communist rule. But this Vatican policy did not make things any easier for the Church in Poland.

A few months before Wojtyla was ordained priest, the Government tried a new tactic – subversion. In a vain attempt to split the Church into two camps, they officially recognised a new, bogus 'Polish National Catholic Church', assisted by a lay organisation called Pax – both of which were designed to provide a rallying-point for Catholics who were prepared to support the Party. At the head of Pax was a highly-suspect character, Boleslaw Piasecki, the leader of the pre-war Fascist Falanga party. He was imprisoned by the Russians, but, not averse to turning his coat, he had offered a deal to General Serov, the Russian Chief of Secret Police; whereupon he was released from prison to set up Pax, with its own daily newspaper (*Slowo Powszechne*) and publishing group, and a monopoly on the sale of pious objects. He became one of the richest, most powerful, and most unpopular men in Poland, disliked about equally by Catholics and Communists.[3]

Perhaps it was partly in order to get him away to a more stable atmosphere that Archbishop Sapieha (to be made a Cardinal at about this time) sent the newly-ordained Father Wojtyla to pursue his studies in Rome. His wartime studies in the Underground seminary had inevitably been sketchy; in Rome he could make them good, study a new language and establish new contacts. There was another reason too. It was obvious now to everyone that Karol Wojtyla was a young man of exceptional talents who should be allowed to flex his intellectual muscles in a very different atmosphere from that to which he had been accustomed.

In Rome he lived at the Belgian College, from where he went each day to the Angelicum Institute to study philosophy and moral theology. During the two years that he stayed at the Angelicum his director of studies was the French Dominican, Père Réginald Garrigou-Lagrange, a Thomist philosopher with a reputation for die-hard traditionalism. Brought up as he was in a highly traditionalist

Church, it is doubtful whether Wojtyla even noticed. What affected him far more was the discovery in Garrigou-Lagrange of a fellow-enthusiast for St John of the Cross, the Spanish mystic and poet who had meant so much to him during the sufferings of the Occupation. Many years later (in *Segno di Contraddizione*), Wojtyla quoted some lines of St John of the Cross which illuminate the idea of God's majesty and transcendence, and of the darkness man must go through to reach Him. The lines he quoted have an exact translation in T. S. Eliot's *Four Quartets*.[4]

In order to arrive at what you do not know
    You must go by a way which is the way of ignorance,
In order to possess what you do not possess
    You must go by the way of dispossession.
In order to arrive at what you are not
    You must go through the way in which you are not.

Such was St John's *via negativa*. Inspired by it, Wojtyla wrote a doctoral thesis on *Problems of Faith in the Writings of St John of the Cross*. Among the jury-members who awarded him the mark 9/10 with the comment '*Summa cum laude probati*' were two future members of the College of Cardinals who would one day elect him Pope. (The rector of the Belgian College where he lived also took part in the 1978 Conclave.) For some reason, however, the doctoral thesis was put under lock and key at the Vatican after Wojtyla's election, and a spokesman offered by way of explanation: 'We do not wish the Holy Father to be embarrassed by the publication of a text which does not necessarily reflect his present views.'[5]

After two years in Rome, Father Wojtyla could speak Italian fluently, and when he went to France in the long summer vacation of 1947 he was glad of the opportunity to improve his French. But his visit had more than a merely linguistic purpose. There were many groups of Polish refugees stranded in France and Belgium after the war, and waiting for the chance to return to Poland. Some of them were in trouble. The French Government which had just managed to clear out its Communist (ex-Resistance) members were now launched on something of a witch hunt and were busy expelling from the Pas de Calais a large group of Polish miners who were stranded there.

Wojtyla hastened to the Pas de Calais to offer what assistance he could to the unhappy Poles, to act as a temporary chaplain and to try and defuse the tension existing between them and the French authorities. He was a man whom both sides found it easy to trust.

As a bonus, he found a lot to interest him in France. There too, the Church was having its difficulties. A report commissioned by Cardinal Suhard, Archbishop of Paris, had found that the French working-classes were alienated and agnostic, and that the country as a whole was as pagan as any far-off mission territory. In an attempt to stop the rot and set his own house in order, Suhard had authorised various pastoral experiments, best-known among which was the worker-priest experiment, which sent a number of young priests out of their presbyteries and on to the shop floor. It was a brave idea, but for various reasons it did not work, and was summarily banned by Rome in 1953. The banning was not the fault of the Papal Nuncio in Paris, Monsignor Roncalli, who believed in encouraging pastoral experiment wherever he could. He had advised the Vatican to let the experiments continue until they either justified themselves or burned themselves out. But that was not Pope Pius's way. He and Roncalli were poles apart, yet it was Roncalli who succeeded him to the papacy – as Pope John XXIII.

Karol Wojtyla, a young and obscure Polish priest, probably did not meet the Papal Nuncio while he was in France. (It is an interesting though unimportant fact that Angelo Roncalli was ordained priest in the same month that Wojtyla was born.) They would not meet until Roncalli had become Pope John and Wojtyla was on the upward spiral as

Auxiliary Bishop of Cracow. And that was a long way in the future.

Wojtyla was interested in the worker-priest experiment, but could not see it succeeding in Poland. He too wanted to help the working man; he had been a labourer himself and knew what the problems were; what it was like to be trapped in a boring, soul-destroying job with precious few rewards. Ever since his days in the stone-quarry at the Solvay complex he had maintained a genuine interest in whatever concerned the working man, not only in his religion, but also in the social, educational and cultural opportunities available to him. So he was keen to learn more about the JOC-iste movement which was rapidly growing throughout France and Belgium – *Jeunesse Ouvrière Chrétienne* – Young Christian Workers (with their counterparts for the universities and schools, the Jicistes and Jécistes). The movement had been started before the war by a priest in Belgium, a Mgr Cardijn. Long before Cardinal Suhard had made his discovery about the alienation of the masses, Cardijn had understood that increasing urbanisation was cutting people off from their roots and was destroying their earlier stable sense of values, disorienting and alienating them. He had set up his first groups of Jocistes in the urban jungles, gathering together young Christians who were prepared to live their Christian beliefs in their everyday work. They had a three-fold slogan: See, Judge, Act. Look at the situation, judge what can be done about it, then do it.

This Young Christian Worker idea was something he could take back to Poland with him, adapting it for use among various groups of people. He was enthusiastic about the idea. Only a super optimist could have imagined such a course to be remotely feasible in the Stalinist Poland to which he was about to return. But then Wojtyla's friends had always known him to be just that.

1. Andrzejewski, George, *Ashes and Diamonds*, Penguin Books, 1965, (first published in Poland 1957.)

2. Wojtyla, Karol, *Segno di Contraddizione*, Milan University Press. By kind permission of St Paul Publications (see Acknowledgments.)

3. Boleslaw Piasecki died in January 1979.

4. Eliot, T. S., *Four Quartets*, 'East Coker'. Faber & Faber.

5. *Informations Catholiques Internationales* No. 532. 15.11.78.

# 6

# Father Wojtyla

IF NEWS OF what was happening in Poland had filtered
through to Rome, then Father Karol Wojtyla must have
returned home in 1948 with a heavy heart, knowing that
once again imprisonments and disappearances had become
'normal'. The 1947 elections had been a farce, political
parties had been dissolved and suppressed, private indus-
tries and shops were being nationalised, and Church prop-
erties confiscated. Poland had become a People's Republic,
the Russian 'advisers' were in control, and the country lay
in the grip of a great Stalinist freeze. Surrounded by red
flags, portraits of Stalin, Lenin and Bierut (even Gomulka
was in disgrace and about to be thrown in prison), peasants
were being forcibly collectivised, and while officials droned
out statistics proving how prosperous the workers were
under Socialism, housewives wandered disconsolately
about with empty shopping baskets. The air was heavy with
slogans, the mind-deadening propaganda which robbed
even the simplest activity of its normal human meaning:
'the train – for – Chelmno – will – leave – from – Platform –
Number – Three – beware – of – bacteriological – warfare –
by – the – foreign – imperialists – the train – from – Cracow
– is – arriving – on – Platform – Number – Two – Long
– live – socialism – and – workers' – unity . . .'[1]
More confident now, the Party was stripping off the kid
gloves and was preparing for open warfare with the
Church. By the end of the year in which Wojtyla came back
home, about 400 priests were either in prison or concentra-

tion camps in Siberia. (Four years later the number was 1,000, about 10% of the entire Polish clergy.) Schools all over the country were being laicised, religious education in schools forbidden, teachers forcibly 're-educated', crucifixes removed, prayers abolished and every religious influence eliminated. In that year and the next, Catholic printing-works were suspended, hospitals run by religious orders nationalised, with many of the nuns and almost all the chaplains removed. Pilgrimages, processions and all public meetings (even open-air parish meetings) were prohibited and the censorship of Catholic newspapers was so stringent that most of the official diocesan papers had to cease publication. It was the era of show trials throughout Eastern Europe: the time when prominent members of the clergy and hierarchy were arrested and charged with 'clandestine activity', espionage and 'immorality'.

In these tense political conditions, amid so many difficulties and restrictions, Father Wojtyla began his pastoral career. He was sent first as deacon to the little village of Niegowić near Cracow, and seems to have concentrated on helping the villagers there to come to terms with the rigours of their life. He arrived in the village carrying only a small suitcase, and immediately let it be known that he would be at the disposal of anyone who wanted his help. If one of the peasants was ill, he would take his place labouring in the fields, and soon became known for his great generosity and kindness. Sometimes, when he had to visit someone in an outlying hamlet, he would accept the offer of a wooden cart in which to travel, but more often, rather than take the men from their livelihood in the fields, he would prefer to go on foot. For their part, they would flock to hear him preach, and, in their own words, they would listen to him 'spellbound and silent.'

He was also continuing his studies. The theological department at the University was still open (the Government closed it down a year or so later) and once again he enrolled as a student. He was still working on the thesis which he had written in Rome on the works of St John of the Cross and when he presented it in the summer of 1949 he was awarded a doctorate in theology. After which, Cardinal Sapieha took him away from Niegowić and sent him to the busy, bustling parish of St Florians in Cracow. 'It was too good to last,' they sigh in Niegowić, 'the very first day we saw him, we knew they'd soon take him away from us. He was a really good man.'

\*     \*     \*

Their loss was St Florian's gain. On the little market square outside their church, a little group awaited the arrival of the new curate. Anxiously they scanned the road by which he would come, looking for the taxi which they felt sure the villagers of Niegowić would have hired to transport him.

They were so busy looking for a taxi that they failed to notice the rickety old peasant cart, drawn by one horse, trundling slowly towards them. Carts were common enough in those days, even in the centre of the city, and no one gave them a second glance. So the cart was almost on top of them before they saw that the young man driving it was wearing a soup-plate hat and a cassock. By the time they had recovered from their surprise he had jumped down and was walking towards them with outstretched hand.

'I'm Father Wojtyla.' He was carrying a small case and a few books.

One of the men had climbed into the cart and was looking puzzled. 'Your luggage, Father?'

'Luggage?' he repeated in surprise. 'I have my luggage here.'

St Florians was indignant: Niegowić had no business sending its curate away without transport and with no clothes to his name. They registered a protest to this effect. But it was not long before they realised that in such matters

Father Wojtyla was a law unto himself, that possessions did
not interest him, and that he was devoid of any normal
sartorial pride.

They didn't know what to make of him, whether to pity
his obvious poverty or be scandalised by it. There was his
disgraceful cassock, for example, a faded, threadbare
affair, covered with huge dark grey patches, which they
suspected he sewed on himself. The parishioners were
mesmerised by the cassock, especially as more patches
appeared on it at frequent intervals. As winter came on,
they began to worry, afraid that he would freeze to death as
he sat hour after hour in the chilly confessional, with the
cassock as sole protection against the cold. It was said that
in the sacristy there was a woollen sleeveless cardigan, and
they looked impatiently for him to appear in it. But time
went on, and the cardigan stayed on its hanger. Meanwhile,
Father Wojtyla would answer the doorbell, greet whoever
was outside and stand talking to them 'for hours' in several
degrees of frost.

At last St Florians could stand it no longer. He must have
a new cassock, and, while they were about it, a new overcoat; though they were not very sanguine about the chances
of getting him to agree to have either. In the end, they
by-passed him and went to the parish priest. The latter sent
for Father Wojtyla and ordered him to accept the cassock,
but he omitted to mention the overcoat. The curate went
back to the people, thanked them very much and said he'd
be pleased to accept a new cassock, but not an overcoat.
The people were not to be put off so easily; they went out
and bought some material, and then, realising it was futile
to expect him to go of his own free will, they tricked him
into going to a tailor's house. As soon as he was inside the
door, the tailor whipped out his tape and took the priest's
measurements before he realised what was happening.
Father Wojtyla was surprised, but there was little he could
do about it.

He never wore the overcoat, though he thanked the

people profusely for it. After waiting in vain to see it on his back, they presumed that he had given it away, and reluctantly they gave up the attempt to protect him from the rigours of the Polish winter. At least, they consoled themselves, his new cassock wasn't full of holes. They grew resigned to the fact that Father Wojtyla was 'different'. The woman who cleaned his room reported that he never seemed to sleep in his bed; either he must sleep on the floor or he kept working all through the night. A little further sleuthing disclosed that he had a key to the church in the pocket of his cassock, and that at night he would go there in search of silence and solitude.

On the whole, such idiosyncratic behaviour endeared him to them even more, and they took him to their hearts. When his name-day, the feast of St Charles, came along (in Poland as in many other Catholic and ex-Catholic countries in Europe the name-day is celebrated rather than the birth-day), it seemed as though the whole parish turned up at the priests' house to wish him good luck. The children would rush up to receive a hug and to say whatever came into their heads, while their elders, more inhibited and embarrassed would shuffle up and whisper greetings in his ear 'just as if they were confessing their sins'. It didn't really matter what they said – it was just a case of showing their affection.

Perhaps because he had continued being a student for so long, he had a particular affinity with the young, whether children or teenagers. They called him Wujek, 'little uncle', and constantly came to him for advice. He never talked down to them or patronised them, and he was genuinely interested in whatever they were doing. He gathered groups of students and young workers around him, organised outings and walks for them, went ski-ing with them, or took them up into the mountains to talk about God. They had a hunger for what he could give, for their own education was now run on strictly Marxist lines.

As the youngest curate and the latest to arrive in the

parish, Father Wojtyla was put in charge of the altar-servers. It was a routine chore, but he took it very seriously, making a point of getting to know not only the boys themselves but also their parents. He went to visit them all informally in their homes. There was nothing of the 'visitation' in these calls, he didn't go to offer instruction or even advice, just to talk and to listen. 'He used to listen,' they say, 'then somehow he had the marvellous knack of putting his finger on the problem. He just went straight to the heart of what was the matter, and then he'd try to help.'

The Poles have a rather charming custom whereby between Christmas and Candlemas (February 2nd), priests go round and visit the families in the parish and they sing carols together. Father Wojtyla loved doing this. He relished every opportunity of singing the hauntingly beautiful Polish carols in his powerful baritone. One evening he arrived unannounced at the apartment of one of his new altar-boys and found a family of six living in the most abject poverty in one small room. The father had been made a chronic invalid by the war, and the young mother was making desperate efforts to keep the family fed and clothed by taking in washing. They were embarrassed at first when they saw the priest, but they made him welcome with a little bread and a cup of herbata. He was appalled by the state in which they lived, and wanted to give them something, but he had nothing to give them. So, by way of a present, he shared with them the story of his vocation, a story which until then he had told to nobody: of how, after the first accident he had ignored the call because of his passion for the theatre; and of how, the second time it came he had had to obey. The memory of that call was, he told them, the 'greatest riches' he possessed. (It was the only time anyone could remember that he had talked about himself.)

Father Wojtyla's reputation was spreading beyond the confines of St Florians, and already his preaching had become legendary. He steered clear of politics (even to mention 'Good' and 'Evil' could bring down the wrath of the authorities), wanting only to persuade the people to trust in God. His voice was a magnet but it was not that alone which drew the crowds from all over Cracow. 'It was because what he said was simple and easy to understand, and because he said it with a blazing sincerity,' remembers a former parishioner. 'You could sense that he longed to take you by the hand and lead you to God. He didn't see himself as a mediator between you and God, he just wanted to be able to put you right there in God's presence. You might say that he was a real shepherd.'

Whenever he preached, the church was packed and over-flowing into the aisles and into the street. Students from the University made a point of getting to the church early so as to get a good seat near the pulpit. He did not dazzle them with oratory, but he spoke straight to the heart of their situation. 'He told us to follow the Gospel message, and that nothing else mattered. I learned from him,' a woman said, 'that God doesn't demand the impossible of us. We do what we can and He accepts us.'

The young priest could hardly have been unaware that he had a following, and the irony of the situation must have struck him; he had renounced the idea of the stage, yet here he was, commanding vast 'audiences' every time he spoke in public. The adulation had its ludicrous side. When, as often happened, he had a second preaching engagement immediately after the first, somewhere on the other side of the city, he would set off at a brisk run through the streets with half-a-dozen or so fanatical admirers hard on his heels, trying in vain to keep up with him.

So great was his appeal that his occasional failure to turn up assumed the dimensions of a disaster. There was quite a drama one Sunday evening when, in a packed church seeth-ing with anticipation, a stranger climbed into the pulpit. The congregation heard the luckless man out in silence, though their faces registered dismay. Then they rushed in a body to the priests' house to demand an explanation, not so much of Father Wojtyla's absence from the pulpit, as of the failure to tell them about it. 'There was,' recalls a parishioner, 'a most unholy row. Everyone was furious.' They had to be more understanding when, during Lent one year, he suffered from a serious inflammation of the larynx and was unable to use his voice at all. It was not long after the affair of the overcoat, and to some extent his own parishioners felt that he was getting his just deserts. 'We hated the fact that he couldn't preach,' said one, 'but we hoped it would teach him not to go around half-dressed in the middle of winter!'

His great friend and mentor, Cardinal Sapieha of Cracow, was no more afraid of the Stalinists than he had been of the Nazis. He had no intention of sitting helplessly by, while religion was being replaced by Marxism. In 1950 he and the newly appointed Archbishop of Gniezno and Warsaw, Mgr Stefan Wyszynski, wrote to President Bierut, accusing the Government of bad faith in its dealings with the Church. The campaign of calumny against the clergy had been stepped up, more institutions had been closed, and the two Catholic weeklies, *Znak* and *Tygodnik Powszechny* had been suspended indefinitely. The Government replied by accusing the Catholic bishops of hostility to the regime, and of treason in the matter of recognising the Oder-Neisse territories. As, in fact, most Poles, including most of the Polish hierarchy, did feel quite strongly about these territories, Cardinal Sapieha undertook to go to Rome and persuade the Pope to appoint residential bishops there. Sapieha went to Rome, but his voice went unheeded; Pius XII insisted that the territories did not lawfully belong to Poland, and refused to put bishops there. Sapieha returned empty-handed, and relations with the Government declined still further. A few months later Cardinal Sapieha was dead.

The death of Adam Stefan Sapieha (whom the people called Prince-Prince Sapieha, because he was a prince by birth as well as a prince of the Church) was a bitter blow not only to men like Wojtyla who owed a special debt to him, but to all the people of Cracow. They loved Sapieha and held him in awe – he was their 'invincible Cardinal', who had known how to stand up to tyrants without fear. In Rome in 1946 when he was made a Cardinal, he had refused to wear the scarlet robes: 'I shall not wear them,' he affirmed, 'as long as my country is suffering.' His people loved him the more for the gesture.

His funeral will never be forgotten by any of those who were present; in Cracow they still talk about it as though it were yesterday, and yet it took place twenty-seven years ago. What made it so astonishing was that, at the height of the Stalinist terror, when processions and large gatherings were forbidden, the people poured into the streets in their thousands, and the Secret Police just melted away. 'They couldn't have stopped us on that day, and they knew it.' There was a huge crowd of men and women, some of them in regional costume, many of them from the mountains, and suddenly they began to sing an old rustic hymn often used at country funerals, 'Jesus Christ, grant him eternal rest', again and again and again as though they would never stop. The Cardinal had wanted a simple funeral, but there was nothing simple in his people's farewell. It was the lament of a region for the passing of one of its best-loved sons. His body was taken from the episcopal palace in the Franciszkanska across the road to the Franciscan church (in whose garden today there is a stone memorial to him, entitled Prayer in the Dark Night of Occupation). From there, on popular insistence, the procession wound its way along the old royal route up to the Cathedral at Wawel, where he would be laid to rest beside all the former Archbishops of Cracow. One of the priests who took his turn at carrying the coffin through the weeping crowds was Karol Wojtyla.

It is probable that, before he died, Cardinal Sapieha had seen that his protégé was in danger of being smothered under a feather-pillow of devotion at St Florian's. At any rate, soon after Sapieha's death in 1951, his acting successor, Archbishop Eugeniusz Baziak (who was not a native of Cracow but had been brought over from Lwow, which is now part of the USSR), decided that the time had come for a change. 'They sent him to St Catherine's in Cracow, a long way from here, so that he could study in peace without having us always interrupting him,' sighs an ex-parishioner ruefully. 'The parish virtually went into mourning. But,' she adds triumphantly, 'he didn't forget us any more than we could forget him. We couldn't always be taking him our problems, but when his name-day came round a huge delegation would go from here, on foot or by tram, to wish him well. And we always had the excuse of baptisms, marriages and funerals. We asked him to them all, and he wouldn't refuse us if he could help it.'

1. Fournier, Eva, *Poland*, Vista Books.

# 7

# The White Wafer

WHAT ACTUALLY HAPPENED was that Wojtyla was given a
two-year sabbatical from parish work in order to study
philosophy and work for a teacher's certificate.

His tastes at this time seemed to hover between two
fields of study which were basically different yet which had
their similarities – moral philosophy and ethical philosophy. He was in fact seeking (and continued later to seek)
for the synthesis between the two, which other Polish
philosophers said was impossible.

The study of ethics fascinated him. As a pupil of the
Catholic phenomenologist, Roman Ingarden, he
developed a taste for contemporary philosophical research
and read widely in phenomenology, personalism and exis-
tentialism, studying the works of Max Buber, Gabriel Mar-
cel, Emmanuel Mounier and above all Max Scheler, in the
hope of reconciling these contemporary insights into life
with the traditional teachings of St Thomas Aquinas. Max
Scheler, a disciple of Hüsserl (the German philosopher
who had influenced Sartre, Heidegger and Merleau-Ponty)
believed that man could not be explained away by scientific
theories (such as those of Freud, for example); scientific
objectivity itself depended on man's subjective understanding of himself and his relation to the world; man's
emotions cannot be reduced to physical formulae – love,
for example, is more than a biological impulse. 'The notion
of love was central in Scheler. It is, as he wrote, "the

pioneer of values", that is to say, the way by which goodness and other values are discerned and discovered. Unless
we love, we cannot know.'[1]

Wojtyla borrowed many of Scheler's ideas, but he made
them his own, or rather he tried to reconcile them with
those of St Thomas. Under the direction of Father Professor Wichra, he wrote a thesis entitled: *The Possibilities for
Building a System of Christian Ethics on the Basis of Max
Scheler*, which earned him a second doctorate (this time in
philosophy) from the Jagiellonian University. The paper
would be reissued some years later (1959) in bookform,
and in many ways it foreshadows all Wojtyla's future writings and pronouncements. The influence of Max Scheler on
his thought cannot be overestimated.

Unfortunately, one year after this, the theological
department of the Jagiellonian was closed down yet again,
a Government action which awoke in Karol Wojtyla a
passion for academic freedom which has never been stilled.
For years he has continued to beg the authorities to re-open
the department but they have always refused. (It remains
closed to this day.) Although several seminaries remained
open, higher theological studies were allowed only in the
independent Catholic University of Lublin (KUL) and in
the new Academy of Catholic Theology set up in Warsaw,
the equivalent of a University, with lecturers paid by the
State.

At this time the Government was busy building up an
organisation of 'patriotic priests' who, like the Pax group,
were ready to support their policies. As this move was
patently designed to split the Church, the Primate, Archbishop Wyszynski, (he did not become Cardinal until
1953) decided to act. Wyszynski was a pragmatist and
although he had no illusions about the Communists, most
of all he cared about preserving the unity of the Polish
Church. In a determined effort to keep the Church
together, in 1950 he concluded an agreement with the
Government in which he accepted the loss of Church prop-

erty, (except for actual churches and priests' houses), agreeing that in a Socialist country, the Church must renounce its rights to private property. This agreement incurred the grave displeasure of Pope Pius, and in any case was soon broken by the Government, who went on supporting the 'patriotic priests' and Pax, imposed a ban on all Catholic organisations, and refused to allow a ration of newsprint to the genuine Catholic publications, *Znak* and *Tygodnik Powszechny*.

Archbishop Wyszynski was adhering to an age-old tradition of royal Poland, that when the nation was without its king, the Primate should manage its affairs during the *interregnum*. He saw himself as holding the nation in trust, and he was quite ready to take on the Stalinists in the fight for the nation's soul. It wasn't the atheism of the Government which aroused his anger, but he never tired of railing against their brutality and their 'inhuman ideology.'

Like Sapieha, he too had failed to persuade the Vatican to appoint residential bishops in the Oder-Neisse territories, and he felt affronted by the failure. At a press conference in Rome he had complained: 'You talk about the Church of Silence, but here in Rome is the Church of the Deaf.'[2] Nevertheless he had no choice but to uphold Vatican policy, a fact which strengthened the Government's hand against him, and made it easy for them to accuse him of betraying Poland's interests.

The new Polish Constitution drawn up in 1952 guaranteed freedom of conscience and belief to all its citizens:

> The Church and other confessional bodies may freely fulfil their religious functions. No one has the right to compel the citizen not to take part in religious ceremonies.

Fine words, but hardly worth the ink that had been spent on them. Even at the time when the Constitution appeared, seminaries were being closed throughout the land – fifty-

-nine were taken over and nearly all the students sent to labour camps. Meanwhile the smear campaign against bishops and priests was intensified and by the end of the year (1952) eight bishops and over nine hundred priests (among them Archbishop Baziak, the Apostolic Administrator of Cracow, and Wojtyla's superior) were in prison.

The Primate protested that the State was interfering in Church matters; and the Government responded by clapping a few more priests in prison. Matters came to a head in September 1953 with the show-trial of Bishop Kaczmarek of Kielce, which was similar to the many other show-trials being held throughout Communist-dominated Europe at that period. Bishop Kaczmarek had been held in prison for thirty-two months without a hearing, and when he finally came up for trial he accused himself of 'crimes' against the State, not only in the recent past, or in the Occupation period, but as much as thirty years earlier! His accusations smeared the dead Cardinals Hlond and Sapieha as well as himself. The result was hardly in doubt: the unfortunate Kaczmarek was accused of treason and complicity with the Germans and sentenced to twelve years imprisonment. When Cardinal Wyszynski indignantly protested, a Government communiqué announced that he would be relieved of his functions forthwith and placed under arrest:

This decision (states the communiqué) has been taken following Cardinal Stefan Wyszynski's persistent abuse, despite several warnings, of his ecclesiastical office; he has violated the Protocol of Understanding, stirred up trouble and created an atmosphere favourable to subversive activities . . .

Unlike his superior, Archbishop Baziak, Wojtyla had managed to stay out of prison, concentrating on pastoral rather than political affairs. Today we might say that he 'kept a low profile'. The time had not yet arrived for him to step into the front line of battle. Nevertheless he was required to do a little minor skirmishing. In 1953, just as during the Nazi Occupation, he went underground, lecturing in secret at the banned Metropolitan seminary of Cracow – in moral theology and social ethics. A year later he was made a professor at the philosophical department of the Catholic University of Lublin (KUL) where he was also chaplain to the students. Father Feliks Bednarski, a Polish Dominican professor at the Angelicum in Rome, was a colleague at the time: 'He was an optimist, a genuine optimist, never happier than when working with young people. Perhaps it dates from his own early teaching days, or perhaps from his time with the Rhapsodic Theatre . . . The students always loved having him around. When they brought a problem to him, he seemed able to bring a new vision to it.'[3]

Following his natural bent for abstract thought, he was beginning to write a good deal, mainly articles and reviews on ethics and moral theology and the problems of young people. His first poetry had been published in 1950 when *Pieśń o Blasku Wody* (A Song of Shimmering Water) had appeared in *Tygodnik Powszechny* under the pseudonym of Andrzej Jawień. Although sometimes he would use other names to disguise his identity (Piotr Jasień and Stanislaus Andrzej Gruda), Jawień was the one he usually preferred. It is interesting that this was the name of the hero of a popular pre-war novel, *The Sky In Flames*, by the Polish writer, Parandowski – the story of a young man who lost his Christian faith, found it again many years later, and dedicated his life to God. Wojtyla-Jawień's poetry was not always religious, though much of it had a moral or philosophical theme, and much of it concerned the essential humanity of man and the dignity of all creation. (It is often said that he is a Franciscan at heart.) He used tangible images to illuminate a much more intangible set of truths.

Unrest was spreading like a ferment. Stalin had died in 1953 but his system was very much alive. Only when Kruschev denounced his predecessor's crimes at the

Twentieth Party Congress did the first major crack in the ice appear, although it was still a long way from breaking up.

When it did finally break up there were those who believed that the Virgin alone was responsible. In June 1956, 16,000 workers from the Cegielski factory in Poznan demonstrated in the streets for 'bread and freedom'.

On August 15th, 1956, the Feast of the Assumption, thousands of people converged, as they always did every year, on the hilltop monastery of Czestochowa in the diocese of Cracow. The occasion that year was special: it was the 300th anniversary of the victory of a motley Polish army over nine thousand crack Swedish troops, and King John Casimir's subsequent vow to the Virgin. Czestochowa had become a synonym for nationhood, a powerful symbol of national identity; and never more powerful than on that day three hundred years later when the nation was once again at the end of its tether. One and a half million people converged on Czestochowa that August day, many thousands of them having walked three hundred or more kilometres from far-off villages and towns. They had come in force to petition the Virgin again – for an end to oppression and for the release of Cardinal Wyszynski who was still under house-arrest in a monastery in the Bieszczady Mountains. The Primate's empty throne was carried in procession high above the heads of the surging crowd, and on it lay a giant bouquet of red and white roses – the national colours of Poland.

In October the Soviet Marshal Rokossovski who had been made the commander-in-chief of the Polish Army, was 'returned' to Moscow; collective farms were de-collectivised and property was restored to its original owners. The situation alarmed Mr Kruschev who flew to Warsaw together with a stupefying array of Soviet top brass. Talks began; Russian tanks moved in. The Poles were demanding a 'Polish road to Socialism' with Mr Gomulka at its head. Kruschev ranted but could not budge them.

Outside the crowds ignited as though by spontaneous combustion; the whole population was out on the streets. Kruschev backed down and euphoria coursed through the people like wine. It was Springtime in October. It couldn't last, but while it did, it was heady. (Alas for the neighbouring Hungarians, their own revolution was mercilessly put down. In Budapest the Russian tanks did not stop on the outskirts, as they had in 'Warsaw.)

Mr Gomulka released the Cardinal from prison, and the Cardinal gave him his full support and appealed to Polish Catholics for 'loyalty to the Republic'. There was much to divide the two men, and the concord between them was never more than paper-thin. But undeniably they were both Poles, they had both suffered prison for their beliefs, and they were both realists. Unless they joined forces at this moment Poland would be unable to survive.

An agreement was drawn up. Bishops and priests were to be released from prison. Religious instruction was to return to the schools, freedom and tolerance were to be restored. The Church for its part had to recognise the existing political situation and accept its economic basis:

> The representatives of the episcopate expressed full support for the work undertaken by the government aimed at the strengthening and developing of People's Poland, at concentrating the efforts of citizens in harmonious work for the good of the country, for the conscientious observance of the laws of People's Poland and for the implementation by the citizens of their responsibilities towards the State.[4]

When the elections of 1957 took place, the Church leaders, for the first time since the Communists took over the government of the country, encouraged their people to vote.

All this appeared to be an excellent deal for the Church. But when Cardinal Wyszynski went to Rome to explain its advantages to the Pope, Pius was so displeased that he kept him waiting for several days before granting him an audience.

*　　*　　*

During the brief ensuing period of Communism without tears (the fragile agreement endured until 1961, then broke down under the oppressive measures of the Gomulka Government), Karol Wojtyla was made a bishop. It was an unexpected appointment, since he had held no special office or ecclesiastical appointment, and he was still very young. At thirty-eight he would be the youngest bishop in the country.

He was canoeing in the Masurian Lakes when the news came through. Next to ski-ing this was his favourite sport, and he loved to escape to Masuria, taking with him a few books and a small portable altar for Mass. As for a cross, it was a simple matter to fashion one by lashing two paddles together.

On this occasion, the messengers from Cardinal Wyszynski had difficulty in tracking him down, and when they had done so it was a very unwilling Wojtyla who went back with them to Warsaw. 'The Pope has nominated you to become a bishop,' the Cardinal told him. 'Will you accept? You know the Holy Father doesn't like to be refused.' (Wyszynski knew it only too well.) Wojtyla considered for a moment, then asked if it could wait till he'd finished his kayak trip. Wyszynski agreed, and Wojtyla returned to a last few days of peace and solitude. The announcement was made three days later, when he returned to Cracow.

As bishop, he visited every parish, said Mass in every church and chapel, went to every monastery, and knew every priest in his diocese.

Years later, in the course of a series of meditations given at the Vatican, he described the role of bishop as he saw it:

I leave you with the picture of a bishop completing his canonical visit to a parish. This parish is not only a part of his Church in the administrative sense; it is the community of the people of God who, whatever their weaknesses, sins and vices, carry within themselves the three-fold mission of Christ and the mark of kingship which He has transmitted to them. A bishop must learn to recognise that 'kingliness', that dignity, in different circumstances: in the young, when they receive Confirmation; in husbands and wives when they renew their vows in the presence of the bishop; in the sick and the old whom he visits at home or in the hospitals. The dignity of man, his 'kingliness', comes from Christ; and it is manifest in the joy which accompanies the bishop's stay in the parish.

The more difficult a man's life becomes – in the family, in society, in the world – the greater his need to be aware of a Good Shepherd 'who gives his life for his sheep'. The bishop visiting the communities within his Church is a genuine pilgrim who travels from one sanctuary of the Good Shepherd to another. Wherever he goes he sees the people sharing in the royal priesthood of Christ.[5]

The people of Cracow were well pleased that Father Wojtyla had been made a bishop, and they signalled their approval by presenting him with an episcopal cross and crozier, together with a mitre from the twelfth-century monastery of Tyniec just across the Vistula. He was consecrated as an auxiliary bishop to the Apostolic Administrator of Cracow, Mgr Baziak, at Wawel Cathedral on September 28th, 1958. Exactly one month later, on October 28th, Angelo Roncalli succeeded to the Papacy as John XXIII, and he was crowned Pope on November 4th, the Feast of St Charles Borromeo, Karol Wojtyla's patron saint. The omens were good.

The new bishop had the letter M and the words Totus Tuus inscribed on his coat of arms, as a sign of his devotion to the Blessed Virgin Mary. (The M was in the bottom

corner of the shield, indicative of Mary's place at the foot of
the Cross on which Jesus died.) And one of his first episcopal acts was to have his mother's ashes brought from
Wadowice to lie beside those of his father in Cracow. It was
an act of filial piety which he had long intended.

Being a bishop did not alter his life-style. He had been
living in a small, two-room apartment since his return from
Lublin, and he saw no reason to make a move. His favourite
mode of transport continued to be a bicycle, the cassock
which he wore was still threadbare and patched and his
shoes were down at heel. He was the despair of his daily
housekeeper. When the latter was taken ill and an
emergency operation was ordered, she protested at being
removed to hospital, on the grounds that if she didn't finish
putting a patch on the bishop's cassock, he would have
nothing to wear next morning!

He had lost none of his capacity for filling a church. But
he had a secret fear that the fact of his being a bishop might
isolate him to some extent from his people, and that was the
last thing he wanted. So he began a practice which he
continued as long as he remained in Poland, and which was
to spread all over that country: *opłatek* parties, something
like the agape feasts of the West. The *opłatek* is the white
wafer of unleavened bread (imprinted with a scene from
the Gospels, such as the birth of Jesus or the Last Supper,
or a picture of the Blessed Virgin), which the Poles traditionally break into pieces on Christmas Eve and share with
each other as a sign of love and friendship. It is a kind of
sacred host, a symbol of solidarity, a secular Eucharist.
Bishop Wojtyla began the practice in church. At the students' church of St Anne, he broke the wafers and shared
them out among everyone in the church, as a sign of unity.
When it became known that he was doing this, everyone
started coming to St Anne's and then the practice spread to
other churches.

For Wojtyla it was not enough. It was all very well to
appeal to those who were already believers; he wanted to

reach out to those who were not. He wanted, he said, 'to bring everyone to the white wafer of love'. So each week he would invite groups of doctors, artists, scientists, lawyers, students, workers, clerks, whether they were believers or not. They would arrive at his minute apartment for a special kind of party. There was no food, but the table would be decked out as though for a banquet, and the evening would begin with a breaking of bread – a glass of wine and the sharing of the white *opłatek* wafers. These were occasions to be treasured by all who took part in them, and it doesn't seem as though anybody ever refused an invitation. Wojtyla knew everyone by his or her Christian name, and the evening would often end in music and the singing of folk songs. He had a special knack for drawing people together, even people of the most disparate kind; he looked for what they had in common rather than for what divided them; and there were few who did not feel enriched by his company.

The intellectuals, many Marxists among them, appreciated his friendship, and his desire to throw up bridges between scientific knowledge and religion. Refusing to believe that the one excluded the other, he could match argument with argument, not as a man who wanted to score debating points but as one who genuinely sought to illuminate – and to learn. Theory could never satisfy him, and he liked to test his views against those of other people. Quite sure of his own beliefs, he was unafraid of criticism. Because in their many discussions he was prepared to see what was good in intellectual positions he did not share, he led many to understand the force of his own. He was the best kind of persuader.

*Opłatek* evenings opened the way for other activities. Sometimes he would take groups of doctors or lawyers to monasteries or retreat centres like Kalwaria Zebrzydowska, with its winding pilgrim path punctuated by forty-two shrines and chapels. One successful surgeon recalls the time when Bishop Wojtyla took a group of doctors on pilgrimage to Czestochowa: it was in the middle of winter and snow lay heavy on the ground. The doctors arrived, hugging themselves against the cold in spite of their warm overcoats. 'But he didn't seem to notice the cold at all. There he was in his worn cassock, with all his attention focused on improvising a Way of the Cross and leading us along it. For me it was one of those profound experiences which leave an indelible mark on one's life.'

In spite of all the other claims on his attention in the course of a busy day, he always made time for the students. To them he was the 'everlasting teenager', one of themselves. 'When he was with young people, he seemed to relive his own student days,' said one of the staff at the University. These young people had grown up in a society which openly despised religious values, so he felt it imperative to show them the relevance of Christ and the Christian Gospel to their lives. He gave Retreats for them at St Anne's (frequently at their request), and often before their exams he would go with them for a day of prayer at the monastery at Tyniec. They would bicycle together to Czestochowa, go kayaking in Masuria or ski-ing in the Tatras, always with time set aside for open discussion and meditation. 'He believes in teaching through dialogue,' remarks a former colleague. 'As Socrates did. And Jesus.' They were convivial times which provided a real release for the spirit. An American woman who broke her leg while ski-ing in Zakopane, was serenaded in the hospital by a group of students. Only later did she learn that the guitarist in the group was Bishop Wojtyla.

One day he chanced to meet a woman from St Florians who had a young nephew, Peter, staying with her. The boy's parents, she told him, had been killed during the war, and he had been brought up by assorted grandmothers and aunts. The boy obviously needed some male company, thought Wojtyla. That evening a breathless young priest knocked on the door of the top-floor flat where the woman lived. The bishop and a group of students were in a van outside, he said. They were off on a ski trip to Zakopane, and as they had a spare set of skis they wondered if Peter would like to join them. Peter didn't even pause for a moment; he was downstairs before his aunt had recovered her breath.

Much as he loved these outings with the students (to whom he was, after 1960, official metropolitan chaplain), he still craved for moments of solitude. Whenever possible he escaped to ski or walk in the mountains on his own, wearing boots, baggy trousers, an anorak and a woollen cap pulled down over his ears. 'Whenever I meet him,' says an acquaintance, 'it strikes me that his is the wisdom of the peasant or of a man at home with nature and with solitude.'

One day, in the Tatras, he sat with a Góral, sharing his bread and sausage, and chatting in the broad patois which was the natural speech of the mountains.

'What do you do for a living?' his companion asked after a while.

'I'm a bishop,' said Wojtyla, still in broad patois.

The man guffawed. 'That's good,' he spluttered, 'you're a bishop, and I'm the Pope.'

Wojtyla grinned and did not pursue the point.

The interest that the young Wojtyla had always taken in the people of his parish had grown and deepened with the years. His studies of Max Scheler and the phenomenologists had added a philosophical dimension to his unceasing efforts to insist on the dignity of the individual in the face of a depersonalising political system. In Communist Poland family life was the one area where people could feel free of State directives, and therefore one area where personal growth could take place. In 1960, Wojtyla's book *Miłość i Odpowiedzialność* (Love and Responsibility) considered in depth this important question of man as an individual, and invited its readers to take stock of their own emotional development and their ability to forge personal relationships. The book was a comprehensive exposition of Catholic ethics, which owed much to the philosophy of Max Scheler. (His paper on a system of ethics built on the ideas

of Scheler had been published the previous year.) It took as
its theme the love between man and woman, the love which
is a mutual self-giving and not a mutual exploitation. Love
is not the same as mere sexual enjoyment. 'Only love can
remove the possibility of one person being used by
another.' In Wojtyla's perspective the greatest problem
which men and women must face in their lives is not social
or political disorder (however much these may hinder personal growth), but the threat to their own moral order, to
their full awareness of the responsibility and self-discipline
involved in their personal commitment to love. *Love and
Responsibility* (it has not yet been translated into English)
is a work of unimpeachable Catholic orthodoxy which
attempts to provide a rational and scientific justification for
the Church's traditional teaching on sexual morality; but it
is not a dogmatic work. As Alexander Tomsky of Keston
College writes: 'The humility of the philosopher who realises the difficulty of discovering the right answer makes his
work "apologetic" in the best sense of the word.'

The book was first published by the Catholic University
of Lublin and received instant acclaim. When a second
edition was brought out by the intellectual group, *Znak*
(The Sign) in 1962 it was an immediate sell-out. It is said to
have prefigured the controversial papal encyclical
*Humanae Vitae* which was promulgated in 1968; but what
Wojtyla's work was underlining more than anything else
was his insistence on the irrefragable dignity and the unique
responsibility of man.

Apart from *Przed Sklepem Jubilera* (In Front of the
Jeweller's Shop), a short work which appeared in the same
year under the name of Andrzej Jawień, and which was
really a dramatised (and extremely well-observed and
poignant) meditation on the problems of human relationships, this was the last book he wrote before being
appointed Archbishop of his beloved Cracow and acceding
to the second highest ecclesiastical office in the country.

1. Hebblethwaite, Peter, *Year of Three Popes,* Collins.
2. Quoted in *Year of Three Popes.*
3. *Domenica del Corriere*, 26.10.78.
4. Joint communiqué issued on December 7th, 1956.
5. *Segno di Contraddizione* (see Acknowledgments).

# 8

# The Second Vatican Council

'Before he became a bishop,' said an old friend, 'Karol Wojtyla played little part in politics. He was interested in people and in philosophy. But little by little his growing concern for people forced him to recognise that he had to be involved in politics whether he liked it or not.'

More than the fact of his becoming a bishop, it was the Vatican Council which effected the change in Wojtyla, and brought him into the forefront of affairs. The Council introduced him to a world outside the restrictive society of Poland, and exposed him to the ideas of men whose experience of life was very different from his own. He is, they say in Cracow, 'a man formed by the Council', 'a man who visibly grew with the Council'. 'The Council opened his eyes and its spirit came to demand his total loyalty; it gave him the world view he needed.' And if such was the effect of the Council on him, then Karol Wojtyla must be a man steeped in the spirit of Pope John XXIII.

John XXIII had become Pope in 1958. He was an old man who knew his time was short, and a radical reformer who knew what he wanted to do with the time that was left to him. The Church of Pius XII had seen itself as the last bastion of Christendom defying the onslaughts of the secular world. John wanted to bring that Church right back into the centre of that world, where it belonged. He wanted the Church to fling its windows wide and give itself a thorough spring-cleaning, clearing out dust and dead-wood and facing up to its own possibilities. 'It was one of John's central beliefs that the Church, while possessing the essence of truth for all time, must be constantly employed in reinterpreting it in the light of the Gospel.'[1] John was a supreme optimist who believed that if the Church put its own house in order, it could then open its doors to the world, and let the Holy Spirit do the rest.

Because he was an old man, he did not delay. In January 1959, at the end of a week of prayer for Christian unity (the great prayer of Christ: 'that they all may be one'), he told his Cardinals of his intention of summoning a general Council. If he expected an enthusiastic response, he must have been disappointed. The Cardinals were aghast: a Council spelled trouble and upheaval. Both they and the Vatican newspaper *Osservatore Romano* behaved as though they hoped the idea would go away if they ignored it. But John would not be stopped from his attempt 'to restore the simple and pure lines which the face of Jesus's Church wore at its birth.' On the Feast of Pentecost in 1959 he set up a preliminary commission to seek suggestions from dioceses all over the world about the ground the Council ought to cover. A year later, when 2,000 agendas had been examined, he set up eleven preparatory commissions to draft the actual documents (schemata).

By November 1960 the commissions had settled down to work, and the bishops of the world were invited to assemble in Rome in October 1962. One month before they arrived Pope John addressed the world over Vatican Radio to indicate the Council's objectives. It was to concern itself, he said (thus disposing of the fear that it would content itself with a little cosmetic tinkering) with the entire human race and its right to freedom, justice and the good things of life. The fortress Church was about to be dragged back into the market place of the world.

\*          \*          \*

Meanwhile, over in Poland there was much excuse for the fortress Church mentality – and also much need for the leavening influence the Council was about to exert. Poland was in the throes of a renewal programme of its own, which, in its initial period at least, was not quite in the spirit of the projected Council.

But then it had been initiated before the Council was dreamed of and was a singularly Polish way of confronting its own situation. In the bad days of 1956 when Cardinal Wyszynski was still in prison, he had chanced to re-read Sienkiewicz's historical novel, *Potop* (The Deluge), which was based on the historic victory at Czestochowa over the Swedish armies, and King John Casimir's vow to be faithful to God and the Virgin Mary, to rid the country of the invader and to free the people from oppression. As 1966 would be the year of the Polish Millennium, when the country would celebrate its thousand years of Christianity, the Cardinal hit on the idea of getting the whole country to renew the historic vow and to base a whole programme of renewal on it, by way of preparation for the Millennium. The bishops took the oath (adapted for modern use) at Czestochowa in August 1956 (even before the Cardinal's release), and priests and people followed suit on the Feast of Our Lady Queen of Poland the following year. A detailed programme of teaching, preaching and study material was drawn up, with a different theme for each of the nine years leading to the Millennium.

The Government couldn't fail to see this as provocation. If the Blessed Virgin was thus proclaimed Queen of Poland, then they were being branded as usurpers. The Catholics underlined the provocation by processing to shrines of the Virgin carrying banners and singing at full throttle, 'The Virgin alone is Queen of Poland'. When the Government announced their own five-year Millennium programme in 1960, the Church reminded them that they were celebrating one thousand years of Christianity. As Trevor Beeson remarked, 'It is difficult to conceive of any other country in the world where a religious programme of this intensity and on such a scale could be carried out for almost a whole decade. In the circumstances it would not be surprising if the Polish Government feared that the millennial celebrations would be chiefly of a religious character, thus offering the world the strange spectacle of a Communist state commemorating one thousand years of its history by means of renewed devotion to the Virgin Mary.'[2]

Whatever the reason, the Government re-assumed its old hostility to the Church; and although the persecutions of the Stalinist era were never repeated, petty and sometimes painful harassment became normal. And although the perpetual sniping between Church and Government was often reminiscent of the Little World of Don Camillo (the cutting of microphone wires when the Cardinal was about to address a crowd; the planning of football matches to coincide with an important Church service), the fact was that the battle was on again for the nation's soul. One side accused the other (quite justifiably) of secularising the nation and sabotaging religious freedom; the other side claimed (with equal justification) that sermons and religious publications were sabotaging the establishment of what they were pleased to call Socialism. Though both knew that somehow or other they had to co-exist or go under, Mr Gomulka, like Cardinal Wyszynski, was convinced that he alone represented the best interests of the Polish people.

Politically, of course, Mr Gomulka had the upper hand. So obstructive measures were re-introduced. For a start, the Cardinal was refused permission to leave the country. (He had already been to Rome, where the new pontiff, Pope John, had received him with open arms.) The clergy were subjected to crippling taxes which they hadn't a hope of paying, and difficulties were once again placed in the way of new church buildings for the new towns which were being built. In July 1961 religious education in the schools, which had been optional ever since the thaw of 1956, was made illegal (though it must be added that no attempt was made to interfere with instruction given by the clergy out of school hours). Confrontation was back in business. Seminarians were drafted into military service, although as students they were officially exempt; articles in the Catholic press and books by religious writers were subjected to endless interference by censors and, even when cleared, to inexplicable delays at the printer's. The tragedy was heightened by the fact that the censors and printers were Catholics themselves and were forced into performing these functions. It was like a foretaste of 1984.

Not surprisingly therefore, although he was making every effort to improve relations between the Vatican and the Communist world, John XXIII was not optimistic about the chances of the Polish bishops being given a visa for the purpose of attending the Council. But the authorities relented in time, and not only did Cardinal Wyszynski and sixteen of his bishops attend the first session in 1962, but also four bishops from East Germany, three from Hungary, three from Czechoslovakia and a full contingent from Yugoslavia. Their arrival was a tribute to the open-minded diplomacy of Pope John who was determined to regard all men as brothers, and who had already made it clear that he considered dialogue with Marxists to be a possibility.

Bishop Karol Wojtyla had been impressed by the preparations for the Council, and seems to have gone there more than half prepared to be changed by it. He was the sort of bishop that Pope John was hoping for. Speaking to a packed Wawel Cathedral shortly before leaving for Rome (he was now the acting archbishop of the diocese, following the death of Archbishop Baziak in 1962), he conveyed something of his excitement and his awareness of what the Council would mean:

> We are all filled with emotion at this time, each of us in a different way. This powerful emotion as we experience it here in this Cathedral, near the tomb of St Stanislaus, Bishop and Martyr, is but one symptom of the vast wave of emotion sweeping over the whole Church in these days. If once we thought that a Council was no more than a historical event signalling some slight changes in administration, we are now sure that it is much more than that. Here and now, in the second half of the twentieth century what we have learned of the Council so far has convinced us that it heralds a real change of direction and a transformation at the heart of the Church.
>
> So we all feel – and all humanity seems also to feel – that this Council will be inspired by the Spirit of Wisdom and of Love, that wisdom and that love which are the greatest hope of mankind today. Man is struggling as never before against attempts to dehumanise him, and his only hope lies in a greater love. This is our intention for the Council.

And afterwards we find him writing from the Council itself:

> There are 17 Bishops from Poland here in Rome. What we represent here was probably best expressed by the Holy Father, Pope John XXIII, in his speech of welcome to us. His words contain a special acknowledgment of our contribution to the history of mankind and of the Church, a contribution

Pope John Paul II embraces Cardinal Wyszynski of Poland.

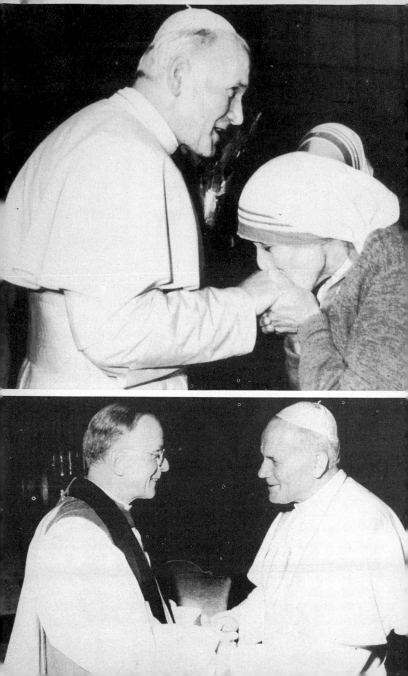

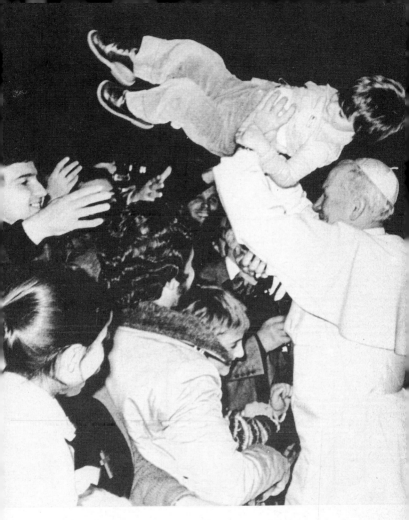

(*Above*) Returns a child to his parents.

(*Opposite, above*) With Mother Teresa of Calcutta.
(*Opposite, below*) With the Archbishop of Canterbury, Dr. Donald Coggan.

Waving to the crowd, he stands on his open car.

immeasurably strengthened today, on the eve of the Council, because of the deep involvement and commitment of the millions of Catholics in our country.

Right from the start, Bishop Wojtyla was noticed. He caught the attention of many of the foreign clerics with his fluent command of languages and his youthful energy and zest. He was, said one of them, 'a young man for whom God alone is the source of human freedom.'

What was remarkable about the Council was the way in which the bishops of the world discovered their voice. They were accustomed to receiving directives from Rome, and they expected that even here they would be subject to control by the Curia. But although many in the Curia misunderstood and opposed the efforts of those who wanted change, in the end they could not win. John's Council gave freedom to the bishops to decide for themselves what sort of Church they wanted, and in spite of Curial manoeuvrings, they used that freedom to the full.

Bishop Wojtyla was not one of the progressives – with his background and experience, how could he be? – but, if he was theologically conservative, he was also open-minded and ever ready for debate. Some of the bishops were at a disadvantage because the proceedings in the first session were in Latin (an advantage to themselves which the Curia hoped to exploit); but this proved no handicap to Wojtyla, who was as skilled in ancient languages as in modern. He took part in the opening debate on the Liturgy and in the next one, on the Sources of Revelation, both of which revealed to the incredulous Council Fathers that the Curia were not after all going to have things all their own way.

There was nothing in the way of concrete achievement after the first session, but ground had been cleared and confidence gained. Before the Council met again in the following autumn, John XXIII had died. His successor, Giovanni Battista Montini, a staunch supporter of the Council, pledged himself as Paul VI to carry on where John had left off.

It was during the second session (1963) that Wojtyla really made his presence felt. By this time his contributions were being listened to with considerable interest, as well they might, thinkers of his calibre not being exactly thick on the ground. On September 23rd, during preliminary discussions of the Constitution of the Church (*Lumen Gentium*) he urged that the Fathers should take care to consider the Church as a whole (the 'People of God') before going on to discuss the hierarchy. In other words he was urging a less clerical approach to the Church's understanding of itself. Such an intervention, coming as it did from a Polish bishop, was quite startling to those who had read in their newspapers that all Polish bishops were dyed-in-the-wool conservatives.

One of the lay 'observers' at the Council, Patrick Keegan, a prominent member of various international lay organisations, had been told by Polish friends in Europe to look out for Wojtyla – 'a very scholarly, very able but immensely human man.' Keegan was not surprised when Wojtyla began to make his mark in this most crucial area: 'He was one of the main architects of *Lumen Gentium*, the document which re-orientated the whole Church,' he claims, and goes on to explain: '*Lumen Gentium* moves away from the idea of a Church as a monarchical pyramid, a grace-and-favour situation, towards a new concept of the Church as a body in which everyone is responsible for the mission of the Church, but each in his own way. What comes out from *Lumen Gentium* is that the layman's job is where he actually is – and that is where he must build the Church. It's no longer a question of helping Father in the physical work of the parish, though that is important and somebody has to do it, but of recognising that the layman's primary job is in the world. As one of those responsible for this crucial document, Wojtyla knows that this change of emphasis is the most important thing that happened in the Council. Because of it, the Church moved on to a new track.'

In a talk on Vatican Radio (26.11.63), Wojtyla voiced his own thoughts about the Council and the future role of the laity in the Church:

At the heart of the organisation of the People of God is a profound awareness of the value of the human person, a value not only physical but also spiritual. We must strive to preserve this awareness of our human dignity, even to the point of shedding our blood, as Christ shed His blood for us. The world is braced for the struggle. The word laity in Polish (świeććy) means 'bound to the world' (świat), bound therefore to that world, with its inbuilt sense of purpose, in which man discovers his own values and realises the tasks he must perform. These tasks are the development of the world and man's own development within it. The specific role of the laity in the Church is to measure up to the times, to make sure that man is allowed to reach his full potential, while at the same time allowing for his weaknesses.

Bishop Wojtyla had a more profound awareness of the realities of the contemporary world than many of the other bishops. He insisted on the necessity for religious freedom for all religious groups in all circumstances, no matter how inconvenient. (The earlier, double-standard attitude of the Church was well illustrated by Louis Veuillot, editor of a French Catholic journal, who, in answer to a question from a gathering of liberal and Protestant deputies in 1885, had said: 'When you are the masters, we claim perfect liberty for ourselves, as your principles require it. When we are the masters we refuse it to you, as it is contrary to our principles.')[3] At the height of the debate on Religious Liberty, when the conservative die-hards looked like winning the day for a defensive stance against 'Error', Wojtyla swept in with a declaration which changed the face of the debate: 'Do not hesitate,' he cried, 'to call for religious freedom. Such an affirmation would be of capital importance for those of us who live under Communist regimes.'

Religious freedom was an absolute, he implied, to which there could be no exceptions. In this he was echoing the words of John XXIII in his final testament to human rights and freedoms, *Pacem in Terris*. Every human being, Pope John had affirmed, 'has the right to worship God in accordance with the right dictates of his own conscience and to profess his religion both in private and in public.' It was a theme to which Wojtyla would frequently return. (In a speech published in *Osservatore Romano* in 1976 he said: 'One can understand that a man may search and not find; one can understand that he may deny; but it is incomprehensible that a man should be told: "You may not believe."')

Indeed he understood those who denied that there was a God; he had, as many of the Fathers had not, first-hand experience of atheism and numbered many unbelievers among his friends. Like Pope John, he preferred to look for the common ground between them, believing that the Church must take man as he is.

It is not the role of the Church to flourish its authority in the face of unbelievers. We and all our fellow-men are engaged in a search . . . Let us avoid all moralising and all suggestion that the Church has a monopoly of Truth. One of the major defects of this draft is that in it the Church appears to be an authoritarian institution.[4]

The draft in question was Schema XIII which in time became the almost equally crucial document, *Gaudium et Spes: the Constitution of the Church in The World of Today*. It was because of his impressive contribution to the debate on religious liberty that Wojtyla was invited to join the Mixed Commission which dealt with this schema, and it was he who suggested (when there was much argument about the wording of the title), that it should be called a 'pastoral' constitution, that is to say, concerned more with life than theory. This enabled the discussion to range over such contemporary problems as marriage, peace, economic development and international organisation. It was he who urged the Council to include a chapter on Marriage and the Family in this document – and the debates in this subject led to a new view of marriage as 'a community of love' which found its highest fulfilment in parenthood.

Schema XIII's final chapter was known as 'The Pill and Bomb', for the obvious reason that it concerned the issues of contraception and nuclear warfare. Working on the committee with Wojtyla was Mgr Derek Worlock (the present Archbishop of Liverpool), who has this diary entry for a day in January 1965:

> In the early hours of the morning Rome had an unprecedented fall of snow, nearly three feet falling in an hour and a half. This had a disastrous effect on the trees, many of which had broken under the weight of the snow; and movement around Rome was almost impossible. Somehow I waded my way to St Peters through the drifts, and was delighted to find the other Europeans and Americans also arriving. The Italians had presumed there would be no meeting and had not ventured out! There was the splendid sight of the Polish Archbishop[5] drying his socks by the stove . . .

'I remember the occasion well,' says Archbishop Worlock. 'I can see him coming in, dressed, as he was always dressed, in a cassock, and he was wringing out the bottom of his cassock and taking off his shoes and socks and drying them by the stove, just sitting there with bare feet, completely unconcerned. He was laughing, and it was the first time I had seen him relaxed like that. It was the peasant side of him coming out. As he was drying his socks, Rosemary Goldie, an Australian woman, came in and put her gloves down, and someone put them on top of the stove, not realising they were made of plastic. Suddenly there was a great deal of smoke and a most horrible smell coming from the stove, and everyone started prodding poor Wojtyla, saying that the smell was from his socks. In fact it was Rosemary Goldie's gloves which had completely dissolved and were bubbling on the stove.'

Rome had caused Wojtyla's horizons to grow, and that growth was mirrored in his poetry. In the first session he was writing nostalgic pieces, expressing the feelings of a bishop bestowing the sacrament of Confirmation on the people of a certain village in the foothills. The following year, the monthly review, *Znak*, published a collection of poetry signed by Andrzej Jawień in which the poet had made a joyous spiritual discovery of a Church whose foundations are in Rome but whose horizon spans the world. Stimulated by his encounters with bishops from the Third World, he wrote:

My dear brother, it's you, an immense land I feel
where rivers dry up suddenly – and the sun
burns the body as the foundry burns ore.
I feel your thought like mine;
if they diverge the balance is the same:
in the scales truth and error.
There is joy in weighing thoughts on the same scales,
thoughts that differently flicker in your eyes and mine
though their substance is the same.

And in this poem, 'Marble Floor', he contemplates the stones of St Peter's Square which seem to him to symbolise the role of the Pope at the heart of the Church.

> Our feet meet the earth in this place;
> there are so many walls, so many colonnades,
> yet we are not lost. If we find
> meaning and oneness,
> it is the floor that guides us. It joins the spaces
> of this great edifice, and joins
> the spaces within us,
> who walk aware of our weakness and defeat.
> Peter, you are the floor, that others
> may walk over you (not knowing
> where they go). You guide their steps
> so that spaces can be one in their eyes,
> and from them thought is born.
> You want to serve their feet that pass
> as rock serves the hooves of sheep.
> The rock is a gigantic temple floor,
> the cross a pasture.

By December 1965 the Second Vatican Council was over, and the bishops went home. But its work still remained to be done, and it was seven years before even the documents were completed. Wojtyla returned to Rome at least twice a year during that period, while at home he set himself to ensure that the Council's spirit would make itself felt in every aspect of the Church's life. Thirteen years later, on the day after his election as Pope, he gave expression to his conviction that the Council embodied a real hope and a firm challenge for all mankind:

> We want to stretch out our hands and open our hearts to all people, especially those who are oppres-

sed by injustice or discrimination, whether it relates to the economy, life in society, political life, or freedom of conscience and of belief. We must reach out to them by all possible means so that all forms of injustice manifest in our times can be brought to the attention of all men and thus be remedied, so that all men may live a life that is worthy of them. This is part of the mission of the Church, as the Second Vatican Council . . . made clear.[7]

1. Johnson, Paul, *Pope John XXIII*, Hutchinsons.
2. Beeson, Trevor, *Discretion and Valour: Religious Conditions in Russia and Eastern Europe*, Collins, Fount Paperbacks.
3. Quoted in *Pope John XXIII*.
4. October 21st, 1963.
5. Wojtyla had become Archbishop of Cracow in 1964.
6. Speech, *Urbi et Orbi*, to the city and the world, 17.10.78.

# 9

# After The Council

IT CAME AS no great surprise to the people of Cracow when Karol Wojtyla was made Metropolitan Archbishop of that city in January 1964. Everyone had expected it, everyone seemed pleased. After thirteen years (since the death of Cardinal Sapieha) Cracow had an archbishop again, the first holder of that high office who was not an aristocrat.

The consecration took place at Wawel Cathedral on March 8th. It happened to be mid-Lent or Laetare Sunday, a day when the Church begins to rejoice at the prospect of Easter. And this particular Laetare Sunday offered its own reasons for rejoicing, as Father Bogdan Niemczewski stressed in his address of welcome:

> We rejoice with you. It may be said of course that we rejoice in your great gifts of learning and wisdom. Yet what really fills our hearts with joy is your simple goodness which reaches out to us all. That is why we rejoice, and that is why today we offer you our love. We rejoice also in your devotion, your spirit of prayer and in your nearness to God.

There, in the historic Cathedral, where kings and Cardinals and poets lie buried, no one can be unaware of history. The new Archbishop spoke of St Stanislaw and Queen Jadwiga and then, switching to the more recent past, recalled the debt he owed to the great Sapieha: 'He put his hands on me and consecrated me bishop. And long before that he had brought my priesthood to birth.' And he went on:

Things eternal, things of God, are very simple and very profound. We don't have to create new programmes; we have to find new ways, new energies and a new enthusiasm for sharing in the eternal plan of God and of Christ, and of fulfilling it in the context of our times. The Council has set things in motion, but for many of us its decrees are as yet merely written documents. I want to awaken the archdiocese of Cracow to the true meaning of the Council, so that we may bring its teachings into our lives.

He was, in fact, thoroughly imbued with the spirit of the Council and for him there was now no doubt that preparations for the Polish Millennium should run in harness with attempts to implement the Council decrees. In an article for *Tygodnik Powszechny* in May, he wrote of the need to allow the work of the Council to light up the understanding of a thousand years of Polish Christianity. In both cases it was simply a question of choosing God – for the nation and for oneself.

There is no conflict between the freedom of the human being and his dependence on God; there is choice, and there is commitment, in which the human being grasps the meaning of his existence and seeks to fulfil it . . . Christ touches each one of us, in the deepest nerve of our humanity . . . The Church is the guardian not only of the deposit of faith, hope and love, but also of the essential freedom of the human beings who choose to share in its work. Thanks to the Council we can understand this reality more clearly. The Church guards the freedom of each individual who consciously chooses God and wants to belong to Him.

Making the liturgical changes demanded by the Council – turning the altar to face the people, switching from Latin to the vernacular, for example – was no more than a beginning. He accepted this sort of change with ease, unlike Cardinal Wyszynski who detested it. (At the Council, Wyszynski had opposed the introduction of the vernacular and had gone so far as to suggest that medieval Latin was part of Polish tradition!) But if the Council was to penetrate the minds and hearts of his people, the changes must go far deeper.

The archbishop was quite prepared to go on living in his old two-roomed flat. His staff protested and tried to persuade him to move to the episcopal palace. He did not, they complained (neither for the first time nor the last), have 'a proper sense of ecclesiastical dignity'. Wojtyla ignored their protests but was helpless when one day, about a month after his appointment, he came home to find that his effects had been moved out. After that he had no option but to make his way to the episcopal palace; it is said that he arrived in person with a pair of skis slung over his shoulder, to the bewilderment of his housekeeper who thought they must be a new type of bishop's crozier.

It must have been a strange experience for Wojtyla to return to that palace, where once he had lain in hiding, hunted by the Germans. Perhaps it was the memory of those times which made him so unwilling to go and live there. But if so, he did not allow himself to be haunted by the ghosts of the past. Within days the palace was buzzing with activity of all kinds.

From the start he knew what he wanted to do; the Council had spurred him on: 'I want to underline the essential question, that of the right and duty of Catholics to remodel the temporal order in the light of the Gospel. This right-cum-duty must affect our cultural, social, economic, political and domestic life.'

Wojtyla intended to make the people aware that the Church was a caring Church. One of his first actions as archbishop was to set up a special ministry to look after the sick and disabled. (The problem of the chronic sick was acute in Poland where so many hospitals had been destroyed during the war; very few could hope to be hospitalised and the waiting-lists were endless. As pain-killing drugs, medicines and equipment were also hard to come by, their plight was desperate.) To run this ministry he chose a priest who had himself been seriously ill and who remained a chronic invalid. (He is still at his post.) 'You're the ideal person for this job,' Wojtyla told him, 'you know what it's like to be ill, and so you will sympathise.'

He also set up a Family Institute which would tackle any possible problems a family might face. This had always been an area of real concern to him; he was aware of the importance of the family and the necessity of keeping it free of disintegrating pressures from outside. Out of his concern for the sanctity of personal relationships, he had written *Love and Responsibility*, and during the Council he had made many interventions on the subject of marriage and the family. There is no doubt that he was a traditionalist in matters of this kind: he deplored abortion (made legal in Poland in 1957, partly as a measure to reduce the population, and partly as one which would alienate people from the Church) and artificial contraception because they struck at the root of what he held sacred. He held his views out of respect for the one area of life which, in Poland at least, was safe from political pressure and where men and women could be free and therefore responsible. (But he was no fool, and he was first and foremost a pastoral man.) Well aware of the many and varied kinds of pressure which affected family life from within and without, he was determined to do what he could to shore up its stability.

In charge of the Family Institute was a woman psychiatrist, D., a close friend who had undergone much appalling suffering. She was a 'guinea-pig', a survivor of Ravensbrück concentration camp who had been the victim of vicious medical experiments. As the liberating armies approached, the SS marked the 'guinea-pigs' down for liquidation, but the Underground movement in the camp determined to save them. D. was shifted around the camp from one hiding place to the next, surviving hourly searches by the SS. Believing herself at the point of death, she vowed that if she recovered and were set free she would train as a psychiatrist and thus help to heal the minds of those whom the war had broken. She kept the vow, though it has not been only war-victims who have claimed her attention. She is one of the people most in demand in Cracow today, with people in need besieging her flat day and night.

Many of Wojtyla's friends had undergone suffering like this, and some of them, like D., had acquired an extraordinary wisdom through it. She was obviously the ideal person to be in charge of his Family Institute. The aim was two-fold: it was (and is) part-clinic and advice-centre to which people came with many different kinds of problem; and part instruction-centre where priests, doctors and laymen involved in social work were taught about the various aspects of family life and its problems. The Centre was open every day, and there was always a constant stream of people using it. The Archbishop made a point of visiting daily, as he did later on when he had become Cardinal. He never begrudged time or advice, and when it was possible he gave practical help. When a pregnant woman showed him the bruises and welts inflicted by her husband, he made inquiries and discovered that the couple and their family were living in a room nine metres square in great poverty. So he gave her money and managed to find a larger flat for them. Poverty like theirs, as he well knew, was often responsible for anti-social behaviour: one section of the Institute was trying to deal with unhappy and delinquent young people.

The work of the Institute was for the whole archdiocese, not just for the city. In the evenings and in their spare time, the doctors went out to distant villages, to offer advice to problem families and to give talks about natural methods of birth control. Like Wojtyla himself, they were opposed to the use of the contraceptive Pill, on moral grounds, it is true, but also on the grounds that it was a potential health hazard of as yet unknown proportions. One of these doctors, who was on Wojtyla's committee investigating the question of birth control and who may have influenced Wojtyla's own thinking, once got into a heated argument with an English friend who was in favour of the Pill. 'You're just a brain-washed Westerner,' she cried. 'At least we know when we are being brain-washed, but you don't.'

It was perhaps in the cultural sphere that Wojtyla could be of most help. Cardinal Wyszynski was suspicious of intellectuals. His own answer to government pressure was the simple piety of the people, the kind of religious piety which had become an anachronism in many other countries: public demonstrations of religious devotion which are all part of the equation that made being Polish the equivalent of being Catholic. With persecution, piety became stronger. Cardinal Wyszynski had come to authority at a time when persecution was at its most fierce and strong and embattled leadership was needed. The vision of the Church which he proposed was accepted by virtually the whole nation. The Government despised it, but they too understood it. Aware that no political body could hope to overthrow the Church, the Government, while continuing its harassment and constant pin-pricks, was also playing a waiting-game. In time, they believed, such simple emotional fervour must lose ground, not necessarily to Communism but to modernism, and if not in this present generation then in the next; while the Church had its eyes on the devil it knew, the devil it didn't know might slip in by the postern gate and demolish the fortress. A truly articulate and informed Catholicism might be a more dangerous competitor to the Government than the banner-waving crowds at Czestochowa. So, for differing motives, pious publications of all kinds were allowed by both Cardinal and Government, while 'progressive' writers like Teilhard de

Chardin were banned by both.

For the most part, the Polish bishops neither encouraged nor discouraged the small group of 'progressive' Catholics in Poland. Since 1957 there had been a token force of five politicians in the Sejm, representing the intellectuals grouped round the Znak publishing house, but outside Parliament they had no platform other than the excellent weekly journal, *Tygodnik Powszechny*, published in Cracow; *Znak* and *Wiez*. Of the sixteen Catholic publications in Poland Tygodnik Powszechny (banned during the Stalinist period) was most closely watched by the censors – 'almost as much as we are', said the editors of the official organs whose every line was scrutinised for heresy.

Unlike Cardinal Wyszynski, Archbishop Wojtyla appreciated the tremendous importance of cultural resistance (the kind of resistance he had put up against the Nazis, both through the Rhapsodic Theatre and his work in the underground university), and the necessity for a well-read and articulate Catholic laity if the Church was to survive the present generation. He was of a different generation from Wyszynski and hardly remembered the days when the Church was powerful and unopposed. An intellectual himself, he was determined to give full support to intellectual groups within the Church. With religious education now forbidden in the schools, it was more than ever important to make religion come alive in the minds of the students to whom it was forbidden.

Although his books were sometimes confiscated, and books sent to him by friends failed mysteriously to arrive, he made every effort to keep abreast of modern thought in the Church, reading as many new works as he could find, usually in the original language in which they were written. He read or acquired many such works on his visits to Rome, although frequently they were impounded at the airport on his return.

Once a month he organised symposiums, lasting one or two days, in which specialist groups of laymen could talk through the problems which faced them in their professions – doctors, scientists, lawyers, not all of them Catholic, some of them even Marxist. With his gift for being able to talk to any group in its own 'language', he always took part in these discussions, to his own enrichment, he felt, but to the disapproval of the curial staff who thought he had better things to do with his time.

Nor did he forget the importance of educating priests in the spirit of the post-Conciliar Church. Never ceasing to mourn (nor to pester the Government about) the closing of the Faculty of Theology at the University, he made the best of the situation by providing a replacement. There were three seminaries in Cracow, one for Silesia, one for Cz estochowa and one for Cracow itself, and he decided to weld the three into a single Pontifical Faculty of Theology, with its own facilities for awarding degrees. The snag was that the Government refused to recognise it – they didn't ban it or even harass it, just ignored its existence – with the odd result that the degrees of the Pontifical Faculty came to be recognised everywhere in the world except in Poland.

All this time preparations for the Millennium were proceeding, and nowhere with more enthusiasm than in Cracow, the cradle of Polish history and culture. Wojtyla loved Cracow and was proud of its long history. He could not, he wrote in *Tygodnik Powszechny*, enter Wawel Cathedral without being profoundly moved by the past and by the continuity of history. Wawel symbolised for him 'Christ, the guarantor of our life, the support of our traditions, a great light for us and for all creation – the light that brings the knowledge of God's love into the human soul.' As a child in Wadowice he had shown an unusual interest in local history and had compiled a catalogue of the historical monuments in and around the town. In Cracow there was still much to be discovered; surprisingly for a city known as 'the jewel of Poland', there was a lack of adequate local history. So historians from all over Poland were summoned to a week-long symposium in the episcopal palace in

Cracow. And not only historians, but representatives of all branches of knowledge, both secular and spiritual. They devoted the first few days to the study of medieval Cracow and then went on to modern times. The consultations and discussions brought to light much that was new and interesting, and shortly after this Wojtyla founded an annual review, *Analecta Cracoviensa* (Cracow Annals), consisting of articles which would further illuminate Cracow's contribution to Poland's thousand years of history.

Always there was government harassment. Though less strident in his dealings with the Communists and more concerned to be flexible than Cardinal Wyszynski, he was never afraid of standing up to them. Right from the start he refused to take part in petty low-level exchanges, dismissing a minor party official who had got through to him on the telephone with a curt: 'If you don't officially recognise that we exist, I don't see how we can talk to each other. Good day.'

Yet he was forced to join battle, constantly having to fight demands for higher and higher taxes, resist campaigns in favour of birth control and abortion, and carry on the endless fight for permission to build churches. In desperation over their delaying tactics, he would often threaten to hold the annual Corpus Christi procession along the old traditional route from Wawel Castle to the market square, a manoeuvre which would have brought all traffic to a standstill for hours. (Corpus Christi is in any case a feast day when the factories are inexplicably empty, and the authorities claim not to know the reason why.) The sad case of the church at Nowa Huta illustrates the tensions inherent in the situation, and Nowa Huta was by no means an isolated example.

The town of Nowa Huta had been built in the early 1950s on Stalin's orders, a few kilometres outside Cracow. It was to be a model Socialist community, the home of new Socialist Man, free of all reactionary influences (in deliberate contrast to ancient Cracow which was full of them). This concrete jungle of surpassing ugliness was built around the massive Lenin steelworks (one of the largest in Europe), and the main aesthetic attraction of the place was a huge bronze statue of Lenin, of such a size as to inspire terror rather than admiration. Everything was provided for the workers of Nowa Huta – everything, that is, except a church, which, being new Socialist Men, they were not expected to want. Alas for expectations, they not only wanted a church, but they wanted it badly, and kept on saying so, to the embarrassment of the authorities. In 1957, in the early days of the October Springtime, permission was at last given and a site earmarked. The inhabitants immediately had the site blessed and put up a Cross as a sign that a church was to be built there. Then in 1960 the atmosphere changed again. The Government had decided to celebrate the Millennium by providing a thousand new schools, one for each of the thousand years,[1] and one of the sites they wanted was the one marked out for a church at Nowa Huta. (To be fair, money and resources were scarce, and by their reckoning a school must have seemed more important than a church.) When workmen arrived to take down the Cross, the people threw stones at them, and then there was a riot. The militia came out with tear gas and machine guns, and blood flowed. In the end (though severe penalties were inflicted on the rioters), the Government decided to leave the Cross where it was, for the time being.

As bishop and archbishop, Wojtyla was engaged in the endless arguments and discussions about the projected church at Nowa Huta, and although he avoided any incitement to violence, he left no stone unturned, mobilising petitions, preaching countless sermons, and constantly being a gadfly to the authorities, pressing them for permission to build. But as long as the Millennium preparations went on, they would not budge. Not until 1967 was permission given to start building – on a different site, and it was ten years after that that the people of Nowa Huta finally got their church, almost a quarter of a century after they had begun asking for it. We shall return to the story later.

The preparations for the Polish Millennium had been marked by a further cause of conflict between Church and State. Early in 1966 the bishops proposed the unthinkable – a reconciliation with the Germans. They went so far as to write an open letter to the German bishops, offering them forgiveness for the past and seeking their forgiveness in return. It was a remarkable and admirable gesture, wholly in the spirit of Vatican II, but it was not a popular move. The Government were furious and began putting up posters which read, 'We shall neither forget nor forgive.' One reason for their fury was that they had always counted on being able to rally popular support against the threat of German revanchism, and if that threat should disappear, so too might the support. There were other reasons: Church leaders were poaching on the Party's preserves and meddling in foreign policy, actually daring to take bold new initiatives without so much as a by-your-leave to the Government. And there was little doubt that reconciliation with Germany, and the establishment of new links with the West, would be most unwelcome to Moscow, opening up, as it did, the prospect of West Germans pouring in money to help the Church in Poland.

It must be recognised that, even apart from the Government, very few Poles were anything but appalled at the prospect of being reconciled with the Germans, at whose hands almost all of them had personally suffered. Nevertheless the bishops made their peace offering, and the German bishops eagerly responded. In Cracow, Archbishop Wojtyla had his work cut out trying to explain to the people of his diocese (which included the town of Auschwitz) that if Christianity meant anything it meant forgiveness, and that the time had come to put old enmities behind them.

As a measure of their disapproval of the bishops' action, the Government refused to give Pope Paul a visa to visit Poland for the Millennium celebrations. But in spite of the antagonism they showed to the Church at home, they were not refusing to negotiate with the Vatican. John XXIII had begun the policy of dialogue with the Communist world, and Paul VI had been pleased to continue it (though many of his advisers in the Curia were far from pleased). Pope Paul's envoy, Monsignor Agostino Casaroli, had been to Warsaw for top-level talks with the Government. It is often suggested that in the course of these talks, Casaroli was asked if it would be possible to provide a counter-balance to the powerful Cardinal Wyszynski, a second Cardinal perhaps (traditionally Poland always had two Cardinals). Someone less intransigent. The Archbishop of Cracow?

Reality may have been simpler; Pope Paul merely wanted to increase the number of Cardinals to 120, and Archbishop Wojtyla, with his fine record at the Council and afterwards, was an obvious choice. On May 29th, 1967, twenty-seven new Cardinals were announced, among them Wojtyla. When he went to Rome to receive his red hat, Paul VI pointedly dismissed the accusations of politicking, referring to 'the sad and troubled situation of the Church in those nations where, under the unmerited accusation of obscurantism and false suspicion of insubordination, its right to a peaceful and secure existence is disputed.'

When Wojtyla returned from Rome to Cracow, there was a Mass and Te Deum in the Cathedral at Wawel.

'It's the last time I shall be a nuisance to you,' he joked to his clergy at the reception afterwards. 'After all, I can't go any higher.' For once he was quite wrong.

1. These schools are now being closed down in great numbers. The contraception and abortion policies, together with low wages and a severe housing shortage, have resulted in a dramatic fall in the birth rate, at one time one of the highest in Europe.

# 10

# 'A Man for Dancing And The Rosary'

'HE IS A post-Council Cardinal,' colleagues say, 'the first Polish Cardinal to stand on the threshold of the second Millennium.'

'Yet he is a man who does not know that he *is* a Cardinal,' says Father Grzybek, a friend of his. 'He is a simple man, full of humility.'

Though he was now a prince of the Church, he made no outward change, continuing to wear a plain black cassock, with no hint of scarlet trimming. His room at the episcopal palace was simple and barely furnished. If anything, they say in Cracow, he seemed to grow more unassuming with each fresh promotion. He still ran his diocese as a democracy rather than an autocracy (which confused and worried the secular authorities), and he continued to keep open house for anyone who wanted to see him.

In fact his daily routine was strict. Up every morning at five, he would exercise first before going to his private chapel at five thirty for meditation followed by Mass. Breakfast was at seven, and then between seven and eleven he worked alone, insisting that he must not be interrupted. A writing-desk was installed in his chapel and frequently he would go there to work. From eleven until one he was at anybody's disposal; each morning between those hours he would be in his office and there was no pecking order of visitors. The mighty had to take their chance alongside the lowly, but all were welcome.

'Why haven't you been to see me for so long?' he asked a woman acquaintance whom he passed in the street.

'Because the Cardinal has better things to do with his time than talk to old ladies,' she retorted.

He 'threw back his head and roared with laughter'. 'I'll expect you tomorrow then,' he said.

But he never wasted time in idle chatter; he might talk to a visitor for the first quarter of an hour, and then suggest that they should say the Rosary together!

In deference to his exalted rank, Wojtyla had reluctantly discarded his bicycle and consented to be driven round by car when necessary (which meant, when he could not walk). So as not to be compelled to waste time while being driven, he had a special lighting system installed in the car, to enable him to keep up to date with his reading or to study essential documents. His driver was fond of him but deplored his untidiness, complaining to a friend of the Cardinal's: 'I feel quite ashamed of him, he's so shabby. Look at his shirts and his shoes. They're a disgrace.'

Walking was preferable, though it made for slow progress, since he always met people he knew and stopped for a chat. Quite often this made him late for appointments, which annoyed his curial staff considerably. He would meet quite casual acquaintances and make them feel 'that talking to you at that moment is what he most wants to do'. It is not surprising, therefore, that almost everyone in Cracow refers to the Cardinal as 'my friend'.

Wojtyla was quick to compassion. A woman whose only sister had just died (and all of whose close male relatives were killed during the war) received a telephone call from him within hours of the death. 'Come and see me tomorrow,' he said, and when she did so, he stayed with her for over an hour. He never failed to answer letters, and they were personal replies, not all-purpose standards. 'He went right to the heart of the matter; he had an amazing ability to find exactly the right thing to say.'

A young English woman, Pat Bains, who went to stay with friends in Cracow in 1968 has a clear recollection of her first meeting with the Cardinal. Her father had just died, and for that and other reasons she was in a very troubled emotional state, as well as being tired from the journey: 'D. told me to sleep late and she would come and collect me for Mass around midday. We would be going to Wujek's Mass, she said. Little uncle! I didn't take much notice, and it wasn't till Mass had begun that I realised that this was a Mass with a difference. It was in his private chapel and D. and I were the only ones there. Priests used to wear elaborate vestments in those days, but he was dressed very simply. He said Mass slowly, and to describe it as prayer-ful would not do justice to what it was like. He seemed to say each word with great meaning and a living belief. Afterwards D. introduced me – her English daughter she called me. He took the hand I offered between both of his, embracing it rather than shaking it. Then he said: "You must stay with us until you are strong again." I remember how moved I was by the genuine concern in his eyes; he looks at you very intently as if he can't waste time on outward appearances but wants to look right inside a person. There was nothing half-hearted or conventionally polite about him, and he left me feeling quite convinced that if I stayed with them in Cracow, I really would get strong again. I made no move to kneel or to kiss his ring – if indeed he had one – and obviously there was no such idea in his mind. He went on holding my hand between both of his without any embarrassment while he and D. talked in Polish.'

The episcopal palace continued to be the centre of much activity – the 'clinics' for married couples, children, delinquents, the sick, were always busy. Wojtyla was particularly solicitous for the sick and the disabled, for their spiritual as well as their physical welfare. He would visit them at home, say Mass for them. (Right up to the moment he became Pope he was beseeching the authorities to allow radio Mass to be broadcast for their benefit. The Church is excluded from the mass media.) And he gave special Retreats for them, arranging on these occasions for them to be brought in cars and making sure that his priests (and he himself) were on hand to help them in and out. Knowing the plight of the chronically sick, and the economic hardships they endured, he set aside part of the palace as a holiday home to which they could come for two or three weeks at a time. Always he insisted that the role of bishops and priests (and *a fortiori* of Cardinals) was not to rule but to serve. Practising what he preached, he was said to put in a twenty-hour day.

The number of his friends was always increasing, but he never dropped any from the past. Old friends from the University and fellow-workers from the stone-quarry at Solvay all came to his house, and his position never got in the way of his relationships. 'A man of the people,' they called him, and, that most telling Polish phrase, 'a man for dancing and the Rosary' – that rare being, a man of God who also revelled in life. Father Grzybek uses another phrase. 'He is a perfect triangle,' he says, 'a man of God, a man of intellect, and a man of great heart.'

That is not the same as saying that he had a taste for luxury. At ease with everyone, he would 'eat anything that was put in front of him', though, when given a choice, he would have the typically Polish sour milk and *kasza hreczana* (a very dark buckwheat from Southern Poland). And wild mushrooms. He liked all things Polish, the food, the customs, the ceremonies, the songs. 'We had breakfast with him on Easter Sunday morning 1968,' recalls the young English woman referred to earlier. 'We'd been to the nine o'clock Mass which he had celebrated at the University church of St Anne, and afterwards he came back to the flat with us, to break an egg with each one of us, which is a Polish Easter tradition, just as they break bread together at Christmas. When he embraced the children, he kissed them firmly on the forehead, taking their head between his hands. The children were completely at ease with him and he talked and joked with them while we prepared breakfast – Polish bread, cheese and sausage, with pickled mushrooms. The last two he ate with relish – I hope he manages to get some Polish mushrooms in the Vatican.'

To reach the flat in question it is necessary to climb eighty-eight stone steps, and most people, even the most energetic, sporting variety, arrive there breathless and gasping. Not so Wojtyla: 'Whenever I opened the door to him, it was as if he had just stepped across the corridor.' Perhaps that is not surprising in one who spent what spare time he could in the mountains. A visiting priest who once went climbing with him remarked: 'It wasn't a particularly long climb, but it was very steep, and as I remember it I had no breath for talking. But Wojtyla just climbed steadily, with unvarying pace and apparently without effort. Even when we came to quite difficult parts he seemed to know exactly where to place his feet, and after a while I realised that, without giving any evidence of it, he had each step planned out in advance. He was climbing with intelligence as well as skill.' Ski-ing apparently required a different set of responses. Known to undertake long and difficult descents without turning a hair, he was, said a friend 'one of the daredevil skiers of the Tatras. He loved the thrill of it, and the danger.'

Once he ran into danger of a different kind: losing his way on a ski-ing trip, he ended up on the wrong side of the Czech border, and was arrested and interrogated for six hours by the Czech security police, who refused to believe that he really was the Cardinal of Cracow!

Wojtyla's support and friendship for the university students never wavered, and they returned his affection. 'He was in my flat with a group of students once,' said a friend, 'and I noticed how he listened to each one with enormous concentration and interest. Sometimes he'd say a few words and they'd listen, but they treated him exactly like one of themselves; he was given no more and no less attention than anyone else, though it was obvious they held him in great affection.'

But students and intellectuals all over the country were beginning to show signs of strain; they were chafing at their lack of freedom, and the atmosphere within the universities was highly charged. In January 1968 a play by Adam Mickiewicz was staged in both Warsaw and Cracow and proved to be the match that lit the fuse. The play was *Ancestors*, and had been written by Mickiewicz as a protest against early nineteenth-century Russian atrocities in Poland – a tabu subject in a Poland which was anxious not to offend its powerful next-door neighbour. *Ancestors* played to packed houses and was met with standing ovations and rousing shouts and cheers, crystallising as it did all the resentment of its audiences, and bringing it to a head. Then, after a few performances, each of which was marked by the same emotional outbursts and wild applause, the play was taken off.

A few weeks later students and academics came out into the streets, demanding an end to censorship. A protest meeting was called in Warsaw – and the Government sent in the militia. Students were beaten up and rage spread like a bush fire throughout the universities. For a moment, Gomulka's Government held its breath to see if the workers would riot in support, but the workers felt that this was no quarrel of theirs: the intellectuals were fighting for ideas, not bread. Once they realised that the workers were indifferent, the Government acted with savage speed, sacking and arresting academics, taking steps to ensure that all avenues of promotion would be forever blocked to them. Students were expelled, their career prospects ruined. (All this must be seen in the context of the Prague Spring, the brief flowering of a kind of freedom in Czechoslovakia, which the authorities in Poland had no intention of allowing their own countrymen to emulate. It is ironic that in 1968 there were riots all over Western Europe, and these were in protest against the outmoded values of Western society; in Poland the students were protesting at the absence of those freedoms so scorned by their counterparts in the West.)

Regrettably, the Church refused to lend its support; the struggle, they said, was a family quarrel between Communists; they did not realise the extent of the left-wing intellectuals' disillusionment with the Party, and saw only that these men for many years had been outspoken critics of the Church.

Only Cardinal Wojtyla was prepared to speak out in their defence, and he did so openly. And when, spiteful in the discovery that many of the disaffected academics were Jewish, the Government began an anti-semitic purge, Wojtyla prodded his fellow-bishops into announcing their support for the unfortunate Jews.

It was not in Wojtyla's nature to stand idly by while any kind of freedom was threatened. And academic freedom was not threatened only by the Government, but often by his own Church. At about this time the government-sponsored Pax organisation was orchestrating a symphony of accusation and innuendo against the radical Catholic Znak movement, the focus of the Catholic Intelligentsia Clubs of which Cardinal Wyszynski was known to be distinctly wary. When Jerzy Turowicz, editor of *Tygodnik Powszechny*, wrote an article for that journal suggesting that it was high time that Church leaders faced up to the fact that there was a crisis in the Church, Cardinal Wyszyński went for him in public. (Turowicz had not even mentioned Poland specifically, but the inference was obvious.) 'There is no crisis,' proclaimed the Cardinal from a Warsaw pulpit, 'except that which exists in the minds of certain Catholic intellectuals.' Cardinal Wojtyla intervened, painstakingly setting out, in a memorandum to *Tygodnik Powszechny*, the duties and responsibilities of Catholic writers in the varying situations they had to face; and he succeeded in calming the situation. More than that, he had to persuade Pope Paul, to whom the indignant Primate had complained, that the Znak movement, far from being a threat, was vital to the health of the Catholic Church in Poland.

The Western press, which loves convenient labels like 'progressive' and 'conservative', and thrives on discord, has always tended to look for signs of opposition between the two Polish Cardinals. The 'Catholic' newspapers run by the Pax group have been only too willing to foster this impression – that the two Cardinals W. are at loggerheads with each other. As a manoeuvre by Pax in its own struggle for power it is perfectly understandable, but it is possible that the Western Press has been gulled. There really is no evidence for the 'loggerheads' view, at least according to the people who should know best, the bishops who attend the episcopal conferences in Poland. If the Cardinals have disagreements they are minor ones, and the two men are close to each other both spiritually and personally.

Both Cardinals are of lowly stock (Wyszynski's father was a sacristan-organist), both are first-generation successes. The difference lies in their experience. Wyszynski came to power at a time when a monolithic Church was being threatened by a secular monolith and could only be preserved intact by strong leadership. Confrontation was almost second nature to him. Wojtyla, less of a pragmatist, more of a thinker, came to authority at a very different time, when the Church of Pope John was re-thinking its role vis-à-vis the world, and the world itself was weary of confrontation. To Wyszynski it seemed as though liberalising influences let loose by the Council were tearing the Church apart, and he pointed to Poland's crowded churches and bulging seminaries to justify his own unyielding stand. He is an autocrat, Wojtyla a democrat. With the help of Wojtyla the bishops have become a genuinely collegial body in which each single voice is heard. But the unity they show to the world is without cracks. Every bishop signs all joint pronouncements personally, lest there be any doubt of their unanimity. In the front line of battle, where every sign of disarray and disunity would be eagerly exploited, it is not only expedient but vital to close ranks.

The unrest of 1968 did not die down, and tensions in the country were growing. The Party leader, Mr Gomulka, seemed to be more than ever out of touch with the population, and this he proved decisively when just before Christmas 1970 he elected to raise food prices by almost twenty-five per cent, without at the same time raising wages and salaries. It was an incredibly inept gesture, showing how little the workers' leaders understood the workers. The fury of the latter spilled over into violence; there were riots in the Baltic ports of Gdansk and Szczecin. Police attacked with gunfire and hundreds of workers were killed. (This time it was the intellectuals' turn to stay at home.) It was the end of Gomulka, and when the new Party Secretary, Edward Gierek, took over, the riots continued until he was forced to bow to their pressure and reduce the high price of food.

The lesson of the riots and of Gomulka's fall was that People's Governments must remember that, in the long run, even they are accountable to the people. The lesson was not lost on Mr Gierek. His Prime Minister, Mr Jaroszewicz, in his first policy speech to the Polish Sejm (Parliament) in 1970, said that the Government wished to strengthen co-operation between all its citizens, whether believers or unbelievers, and he hoped that this policy would meet with understanding from the Catholic clergy and laity. It was an olive branch and when, at long last, West Germany signed a treaty with Poland which recognised the post-war frontiers, and the Vatican hastened to appoint residential bishops to the western territories and incorporate the new dioceses firmly within the Polish Church, the barometer seemed set fair for what the Government called 'normalisation' of relations between Church and State – though it must be admitted that both had a very different idea of what the word meant. By and large there was a tacit understanding that if the Church would not actively oppose

Socialism, the State would acknowledge its role as a useful moral and educational force in society.

So once again there was a thaw, and, as with the earlier thaw, it would last only a few years. Relations between the Church and the State seemed to have a see-saw momentum of their own.

# 11

# 'This Magnificent Fool'

THE OTHER 'NORMALISATION', that of relations between Poland and West Germany, was a great joy to Cardinal Wojtyla. The new treaty set the seal on the bishops' 1966 initiative, and since that time there have been many official meetings between Poles and Germans. (Just last year, 1977, Cardinal Wyszynski visited West Germany and said Mass in the former concentration camp of Dachau.) The German section of Pax Christi (an organisation for peace) and the Polish Znak group have held joint seminars alternately in Germany and Poland every two years, and those on Polish soil usually take place at – Auschwitz.

Auschwitz is only a short distance from Cracow. Beyond doubting, the worst hell-on-earth ever devised by man (it had the capacity to exterminate 60,000 people every day), it is nevertheless seen by Wojtyla today as a sign of hope. The reason – a Polish Franciscan priest called Maximilian Kolbe, who gave his life in Auschwitz to save that of another, and who on October 17th, 1971 was beatified in Rome. (The first day of Pope John Paul II's pontificate, October 17th, 1978, was thus on the anniversary of this event, a fact which would not escape his attention.) The occasion of the Beatification of Father Maximilian was an occasion of great joy – and of profound reconciliation. It was attended by almost all the German bishops (or their representatives) and by four or five thousand German laypeople. The Germans had given financial assistance to make the celebrations possible, and there were many poig-

nant scenes of reconciliation, many Masses attended by
Poles and Germans together, and a general recognition
that old wounds were being healed within the Church, the
sign and token of forgiveness.

Speaking at Auschwitz in 1972, on the first anniversary
of Father Kolbe's beatification in front of a large audience
from many nations, many of them yet again from Germany,
Cardinal Wojtyla said:

> Auschwitz is a place that has a threatening significance
> not only for our nation but for the whole race. It is
> significant in the sheer scale of its horrifying contempt
> for the human person, the extent to which it witnessed
> the destruction of one human being by another. It is a
> place in which the command to love was replaced by the
> imperative of hatred. Is this any less true today? Has the
> liquidation of Auschwitz camp meant the disappearance
> of what it stood for?
>
> But God's Providence manifested itself at last,
> towards the end of that terrible time of trial of which
> Auschwitz has remained the ultimate symbol. The life
> and death of Maximilian Kolbe show the power of love
> victorious over hatred, and of the power of the human
> spirit to survive.[1]

The story of Father Kolbe is familiar throughout Poland.
He was a remarkable man not only in his death, and his
influence on Cardinal Wojtyla was profound. As a priest he
was very well-known in Poland, his monastery at
Niepokalanów (built by himself and his friars in 1927)
being one of the largest in the world (some say *the* largest),
and the centre of much and varied activity. Niepokalanów
was completely self-supporting, its 762 inhabitants com-
prising doctors, dentists, farmers, mechanics, tailors, buil-
ders, printers, gardeners, shoemakers and cooks. (Later on
when Father Maximilian acquired a fire brigade he turned
some of his monks into firemen as well.) It was a seminary,

a mission-house, a printing establishment, a radio station; there seemed no end to its possibilities. Father Maximilian was the guiding spirit: the success of a monthly magazine (its circulation went from 5,000 to 70,000 to 750,000) encouraged him to instal ultra-modern machinery in his printing establishment and to adopt the latest techniques of type-setting, photogravure and binding. By 1935 he had launched a daily Catholic newspaper, and in the few short years of its existence it became Poland's best-selling newspaper, 137,000 copies being printed on weekdays and 225,000 on Sundays. And Maximilian did not rest there: intent on the Church being able to use all the means of social communication, he set up a radio station whose signature tune, the Lourdes hymn, was played by (of course) the friars' own orchestra. And that was when he decided that Niepokalanów must have its own fire brigade, since all the valuable equipment needed to be protected.

Father Maximilian went to Japan and set up a Niepokalanów there. (The name means 'City of the Immaculate' and expressed his lifelong devotion to the Virgin Mary.) It said something for his determination that, in spite of knowing no word of Japanese, exactly one month after the arrival of himself and four other friars he had acquired a printing press and was distributing a magazine. (The Archbishop of Nagasaki, learning that Father Maximilian possessed two doctorates, asked him to take the vacant chair of philosophy in the diocesan seminary in exchange for a licence to start printing.)

Leaving Japan he sailed to Malabar where he founded a third Niepokalanów; and later still, travelling through Russia, he dreamed of setting up yet another, planning to publish his magazine in Russian. He had studied the language and had a fair knowledge of Marxist literature; and like John XXIII – and Cardinal Wojtyla – he looked for the good elements even in the systems he believed to be evil.

In 1936 he was recalled to Poland; his health which had always been bad (he suffered from tuberculosis) had deteriorated badly. He was racked by violent headaches and was covered with abscesses. But these things were only pinpricks. The real martyrdom was waiting for him in Poland.

By September 13th, 1939, Niepokalanów had been occupied by the invading Germans and most of its inhabitants deported to Germany. Among them was Father Maximilian. But that particular exile was short-lived and on December 8th (the feast of the Immaculate Conception of the Virgin) the prisoners were set free. Then began a frenzy of activity. Father Maximilian organised a shelter for 3,000 Polish refugees, among them 2,000 Jews. 'We must do everything in our power to help these unfortunate people who have been driven from their homes and deprived of even the most basic necessities. Our mission is among them.' The friars shared everything they had with the refugees. They housed, fed and clothed them, and brought all their machinery into use in their service.

Naturally they came under suspicion. Early in 1941, in the very last edition of his magazine, *Knight of the Immaculate*, Father Maximilian put pen to paper and laid himself open to arrest: 'No one in the world can change Truth,' he wrote. 'What we can do and should do is to seek Truth and to serve it when we have found it. The real conflict is the inner conflict. Beyond armies of occupation and the hecatombs of extermination camps, there are two irreconcilable enemies in the depth of every soul: good and evil, sin and love. And what use are the victories on the battle-field if we ourselves are defeated in our innermost personal selves?'

On February 17th, 1941 he was arrested and sent to the infamous Pawiak prison in Warsaw. Here he was singled out for special ill-treatment. A witness tells us that in March of that year an SS guard, seeing this man in the Franciscan habit girdled with a rosary asked if he believed in Christ. When the priest replied 'I do,' the guard struck him. The SS man repeated the question several times, and, always

receiving the same answer, went on beating him mercilessly. Shortly afterwards his Franciscan habit was taken
away and a prisoner's garment substituted.

At Auschwitz, whence he was deported on May 28th,
Father Maximilian received the striped convict garment
and was branded with the number 16670. He was put to
work immediately carrying blocks of stone for the construc-
tion of a crematorium wall. On the last day of May he was
assigned with other priests to the Babice section which was
under the direction of 'Bloody' Krott, an ex-convict. 'These
men are layabouts and parasites,' the Commandant said to
Krott, 'get them working.' Krott forced the priests to cut
and carry huge tree trunks. The work went on all day
without a stop and had to be done at the double – spurred
on by vicious blows from the guards. Despite his one lung,
Father Maximilian accepted the work and the blows with
amazing calm, especially in view of the fact that Krott
conceived a violent hatred for the Franciscan and gave him
even heavier tasks than the others. Sometimes his colleagues would try to come to his aid, but he refused to put
them in danger. 'No,' he said, 'Mary gives me strength. All
will be well.'

One day Krott found some of the heaviest planks in the
vicinity and personally loaded them on to the Franciscan's
back, ordering him to run with them. When he collapsed,
Krott kicked him in the stomach and face and had his men
give him fifty lashes. When the priest lost consciousness
Krott flung him down into the mud and left him for dead.
But his companions managed to smuggle him to the Revier,
the camp hospital. Although he was suffering greatly, he
secretly heard confessions in the hospital and spoke to the
other inmates about the love of God. When food was
brought in and everyone struggled to get his place and be
sure of a portion, Father Kolbe stood aside, so that frequently there would be none left for him. At other times he
shared his meagre ration of soup or bread with others.
Once he was asked if such self-denial didn't amount to folly

in a place where every man had to struggle to survive, and he answered: 'Every man has an aim in life. For most men it is to return home to their wives and families. For my part, I want to give my life for the good of all men.'

Men gathered in secret to hear his words of love and encouragement, but it was his example which counted for most. Father Zygmunt Rusczak remembers: 'Each time I saw Father Kolbe in the courtyard I felt within myself an extraordinary effusion of his own goodness. Although he wore the same ragged clothes as the rest of us, with the same tin can hanging from his belt, one always forgot this wretched exterior and was conscious only of the charm of his inspired countenance and of his radiant holiness.'

One day in July, a prisoner apparently escaped from Auschwitz, and the camp authorities decreed that ten men must die as a reprisal – starved to death in the dreaded, windowless underground Bunker. (The dreadful irony is that the 'escapee' was later found drowned in a camp latrine, so the terrible reprisals were quite unnecessary.) The prisoners were paraded in the blazing midday sun and ten victims were selected at random. One of them, Franciszek Gajowniczek, cried out in a despairing voice, 'My wife, my children, I shall never see them again.' Then amid general astonishment a man stepped out from the ranks and offered to take Gajowniczek's place. He was prisoner 16670, Maximilian Kolbe. The SS man, 'Butcher' Fritsch, did not care who went to the Bunker, so long as there were ten of them, so he nodded. 'Who are you?' he asked carelessly. 'I am a Catholic priest,' was the reply.

The story of course does not have a happy ending. Bruno Borgowiec, an assistant to the janitor and an interpreter in the underground Bunkers, was an actual eye-witness:

In the cell of the poor wretches there were daily loud prayers, the rosary and singing, in which prisoners from neighbouring cells also joined. When no SS men were in the Block I went to the Bunker to talk to the men and comfort them. Fervent prayers and songs to the 'holy Mother of the Unhappy' resounded in all the corridors of the Bunker. I had the impression of being in a church. Father Kolbe was leading and the prisoners responded in unison. They were often so deep in prayer that they did not even hear that inspecting SS men had descended to the Bunker; and the voices fell silent only at the loud yelling of their visitors. When the cells were opened the poor wretches cried loudly and begged for a piece of bread and for water which they did not receive. If any of the stronger ones approached the door he was immediately kicked in the stomach by the SS men, so that falling backwards on the cement floor he was instantly killed; or he was shot to death . . . Father Kolbe bore up bravely, he did not beg and did not complain but raised the spirits of the others . . .

Since they had grown very weak prayers were now only whispered. At every inspection, when almost all the others were now lying on the floor, Father Kolbe was seen kneeling or standing in the centre as he looked cheerfully in the faces of the SS men. Two weeks passed in this way. Meanwhile, one after another they died, until only four were left, including Father Kolbe. This the authorities felt was too long; the cell was needed for new victims. So one day they brought in the head of the sick-quarters, a German, a common criminal called Bock, who gave each in his turn an injection of carbolic acid in the vein of the left hand. Father Kolbe with a prayer on his lips himself gave his arm to the executioner. Unable to watch this I left the cell under the pretext of work to be done. Immediately after the SS men had left I returned to the cell, where I found Father Kolbe leaning in a sitting position against the back wall with his eyes open and his head drooping sideways. His face was calm and radiant.

The heroism of Father Kolbe went echoing through

Auschwitz and beyond. In that desert of hatred he had sown love. His death, declared Jerzy Bielecki, was 'a shock filled with hope, bringing new life filled with strength . . . It was like a powerful shaft of light in the darkness of the camp.'

After the war, newspapers all over the world began carrying articles about this 'saint for our times', 'saint of progress', 'giant of holiness'. Cures were claimed through him. 'The life and death of this one man alone,' wrote the Polish bishops, 'is proof and witness of the fact that God can overcome the greatest hatred, the greatest injustice, even death itself.' The demands for his beatification became insistent, and eventually proceedings started in 1947. When all the usual objections had been overcome, the promoter spoke of 'the charm of this magnificent fool'.

When Maximilian Kolbe was beatified Franciszek Gajowniczek, the man he had saved, was present. Cardinal Wojtyla attended the ceremony in Rome and later addressed a Press conference. He fastened on to the fact that Father Kolbe had replied to Fritsch, 'I am a Catholic priest.'

So it was as a Catholic priest that he accompanied his wretched flock of nine men condemned to death. It was not a question of saving the life of the tenth man – he wanted to help those nine to die. From the moment that the dreadful door clanged shut on the condemned men, he took charge of them, and not just them but others who were dying of hunger in cells nearby, and whose demented cries caused anyone who approached to shudder . . . It is a fact that from the moment Father Kolbe came into their midst, those wretched people felt a protective presence, and suddenly their cells, in which they awaited the ghastly final dénouement, resounded with hymns and prayers. The SS themselves were astounded: '*So was haben wir nie gesehen*' (we never saw anything like it before), they said . . .

At a time when so many priests all over the world are fretting about their 'identity', Father Maximilian Kolbe gives the answer, not with theological argument, but with his own life and death. He wished, like his Master, to prove that 'greater love hath no man than this . . .' – the ultimate test for a follower of Christ. We cannot all be heroes, but is it not a sign of failure if we simply refuse to be tested? . . .

Father Maximilian died in an age of fury and contempt, in which men were reduced to the level of robots, lower even than slaves. The nightmare memory of the concentration camps is slowly fading; the young know scarcely anything about them . . . but the survivors of that period know only too well that under a totalitarian system the human person is degraded, humiliated and mocked. Against that background only hatred can flourish. A survivor once said to me: 'I hate them, because they taught me to hate.'

But the astonishing thing to which innumerable witnesses testify is that Maximilian Kolbe knew nothing of hatred. He looked at executioners and victims alike with the same clear gaze, to the point where even the most sadistic turned away, saying, 'Do not look at us like that.' This man, who was branded with the number 16670, won that most difficult of victories, that of a love which absolves as it forgives . . .

It is, therefore, no chance, but a sign of the times, that this priest who died in 1941 at the age of forty-seven in a famine-hole at Auschwitz should today be pronounced 'Blessed', during this Synod which has as its aim the definition of the priestly ministry. To all the more or less abstract questions which have been asked, here is one concrete answer, this man of flesh and blood who carried out his commitment to the end . . .

With such a powerful exemplar of fidelity unto death to admire, Cardinal Wojtyla, who had much in common with the Franciscan, could have little sympathy with the priests who at that time were renouncing their ministry in droves. Maximilian Kolbe was the ideal of what a priest should be, a modern 20th century priest, a man who embodied in his own person the love that Christ showed towards all men. Wojtyla himself had no doubts. 'What is almost unusual at the present time,' said a friend, 'is that he is a priest who actually wants to be a priest. You sense that he is secure, and that makes you feel secure too.'

1. From *Tygodnik Powszechny*, 25.9.72.
All the material on Father Kolbe in this chapter is from a small footnote written by myself for the Catholic Truth Society, on the occasion of his beatification in 1971.

# 12

# Synods

WHAT DOES IT mean to be a Christian in our times? To be a witness to Christ in the world of today? The Vatican Council had confronted the Church with those questions, and Karol Wojtyla, for one, was determined to try to find an answer. For this reason he decided to hold a Synod, or consultative council, in his own archdiocese. Cracow had been preparing for a Synod in 1939 when war broke out, and since then the question had not arisen. Wojtyla decided that his Synod would be different from all previous ones. In the past they had been clerical affairs, assemblies of priests gathered together to pass resolutions on agreed topics. This one would be 'pastoral' – since John XXIII had conceived of the Council itself as 'pastoral'; it would involve all the people, harness the energy of the entire community, 'so that we may work together in the light of faith, enriching, deepening and strengthening that faith in every person of good will.' 'The times in which we live,' he said, 'are an agonising test of faith. I am only too well aware that man's loss of belief is disturbing the roots of his being, in our times more than in previous generations. St John spoke of "the victory which overcomes the world, our faith . . ." and we Christians of the second half of the twentieth century have a deep longing for that victory and we shall work towards it with all our strength.'

Cardinal Wojtyla wanted his Synod to transform the life of his people. Once before, when he was consecrated archbishop, he had said, 'We have no need of programmes . . .

we need new ways, new energies, a new determination.'
This was what he was seeking now – new ways to bring the
spirit of God alive. His Synod was not to be a once-for-all
affair; in fact he expected it to go on for ever. Officially,
however, it was given an eight year span; that is to say, from
May 1971 until the end of May 1979, the 900th anniversary
of St Stanislaus' death.

St Stanislaus is the patron saint of Poland, but nowhere is
he more venerated than in his home town of Cracow, of
which he once was bishop and in whose Cathedral he is
buried. The story goes that in 1079 Bishop Stanislaw
denounced in no uncertain terms the immorality of King
Boleslaw the Bold, and the king promptly had the bishop
killed by his knights. Pope Gregory VII was furious and
Boleslaw was both excommunicated and driven into exile,
while the martyred Stanislaus was canonised. Every succeeding Polish king had to walk barefoot in sackcloth to
kneel at the Saint's tomb and beg forgiveness for the
monarch's crime. History is interwoven with legend and
nobody will ever really know what happened. There must
be at least a suspicion that the accepted version owes something to the famous story of Henry II of England and
Thomas à Becket. (Who will rid me of this turbulent
priest?) But mere historical accuracy fades into insignificance beside the potency of the symbolism. St Stanislaus
played a vital role in the thirteenth and fourteenth centuries as the symbol of Polish unity, and although from the
nineteenth century onwards historians have ventured to
suggest that he might indeed have been a turbulent priest
who meddled in politics and received his just deserts, his is
still a name to be conjured with in Poland and may not be
lightly derided. Like Thomas à Becket he symbolises the
right of the individual to criticise those in authority, and so
he is an early champion of human rights.[1]

Cardinal Wojtyla is well aware of the ambiguities sur-
rounding the story, but regards the symbolism as important
and shares in the general devotion to Stanislaus. The 900th

anniversary of the Saint's death would be a fitting time to mark the end of the Synod. 'We must bear witness to our faith in Jesus Christ as clearly in the twentieth century as in the eleventh,' he wrote in *Tygodnik Powszechny*, 'not only by remembering St Stanislaus but by bearing the same kind of Christian witness in our own lives.'

To make the people aware of the work of the Vatican Council, he set up informal study groups in every parish. Each of these had one member who was a priest, but he was not in charge, he was there only to offer a theological perspective. The original groups were large, but these soon split into much smaller groups, all of them intent on studying the Council documents.

'How many groups do you hope to have?' a Catholic journalist asked the Cardinal at the outset.

'Well,' he replied, 'it may be optimistic of me, but I hope there may be as many as fifty.'

Today (1978) nearly five hundred groups are registered and at least two-thirds of this number are thoroughly active. They represent a considerable lay force in the Church, an admirable substitute (if that is the word) for the Catholic organisations which are officially banned. There is one central diocesan commission which meets once a year, and responsible to it are sub-commissions representing laity, clergy and religious orders (and also specialist commissions of experts in sociology, psychology, medicine etc). The Laity Commission has a layman in charge, is composed mainly of laymen, and its chairman is a member (the only lay member) of the central commission.

This central body prepares documents for general discussion and the study groups choose any one of these, discuss it and submit their opinion. It is a procedure which enables lay people to exercise an unprecedented amount of influence over decision-making in their diocese. For example, the first document drawn up was on the subject of Evangelisation, the spreading of the Gospel. The cleric who wrote the original document produced a vague sermon, a typical document, which would have been normal enough in pre-conciliar days. The study groups gave it a hammering, and submitted a detailed criticism. The document was returned to the central commission and was re-written in the way the study groups had suggested.

Not that this new freedom came easily at first. Laypeople in Poland (and not only in Poland) had no tradition of arguing with the clergy (which in the past had meant arguing with Rome), and the maxim *Roma locuta, causa finita* (when Rome has uttered, don't argue) was deeply ingrained in the Catholic psyche. Catholics had lost the habit of discussing serious matters openly and freely; such things were safer left to the professionals. So at the early meetings organised by Cardinal Wojtyla, the naturally talkative talked far too much, while the others didn't say a word. Obviously this would not do. A rule was therefore laid down: everyone who attended must say something, but nobody must talk for more than five minutes. It was amazing how fruitful the discussions became.

Everyone took part. It is easy to imagine that no one but the intellectuals in the Church could be bothered, but the facts belie that theory. People came from all walks of society. In one group there was a woman from a small country hamlet near Auschwitz. The question being asked of the group was: 'When do you discuss the means of spreading the gospel?' When her turn came she replied: 'It's what we talk about while plucking the goose feathers to make quilts.'

Once a year the general Synod meets in the Cathedral, and at the same time there are working parties and voting meetings at the monastery at Tyniec. Invited to these are representatives of the various deaneries and one or two members from each study group. The names have to be proposed well in advance, so that the Cardinal may send a personal invitation to each one. But there has been an unforeseen snag: one of the rules is that there must be more clergy than laymen, but in the last few years the Commission's secretary has had difficulty in keeping the balance. So many laypeople want to attend that it is almost impossible to find enough priests. It seems as though Cardinal Wojtyla has brought the laity into the Church with a vengeance.

\*        \*        \*

Since the Council, he had frequently returned to Rome to take part in the post-Conciliar Commission on the Laity. In January 1967 the first Council for the Laity was set up. Its president and secretaries were ecclesiastics, but they were there in a consultative capacity; only the lay members had a vote. Patrick Keegan, who was a lay member of this Council, found that Wojtyla had a natural understanding of the relationship between priest and layman. 'He understood that in certain matters the layman must be allowed to decide. In those matters the priest's role is that of tutor, who may suggest but not control.'

In Rome his tall, slightly stooped figure was becoming a familiar sight. He walked with slow, deliberate tread, never hurrying, head down as though he were lost in contemplation. 'You could see him walking along,' says Archbishop Worlock, 'with pursed lips, eyes screwed up, brow puckered, obviously concentrating on some profound thought. Then suddenly he would recognise a friend and a great light would come into his eyes, and his whole face would come alive.

'He is much more withdrawn than people seem to imagine,' continues the Archbishop. 'Those who suggest that he's the life and soul of the party and always the centre of a crowd have got it quite wrong. When he is really relaxing he will lie back, throw back his head and burst into a Polish folk-song. But in a group of people, during a break in a meeting (the *pausa coca-cola*, the Italians call it) he will most probably be in a corner talking quietly to someone, or wandering about with his head bent, or even just sitting alone with a book of prayers or poetry. He's not the sort to have everyone crowding around him. He has a tremendous feeling for popular devotion and community worship, yet that is balanced by a withdrawn person's spirituality.'

'In all these years,' says Patrick Keegan, 'he was learning about the nitty-gritty of the Church's work in Rome. He's not a man who has always been at the receiving end of prepared documents; he's been involved in all the preparations himself. He knows all the tensions, and he knows people as they are, hot-tempered and shouting at each other, which normally people at the top don't have the chance of knowing. He's experienced it all for himself, and that will be a great strength.'

The 1971 Synod, during which the beatification of Maximilian Kolbe had taken place, was not the first one which Cardinal Wojtyla had attended. He had been chosen by the Polish bishops to represent them at the two previous Rome Synods of 1967 and 1969 (as well as at the later ones of 1974 and 1977). At the 1967 Synod, hopes had run high that Pope Paul might establish the Church as a genuinely democratic institution in which Peter might share his authority with the other apostles. The Dogmatic Constitution *Lumen Gentium* had referred to the collegiality of the bishops, which had given rise to hopes of an end to the old monarchical pyramid, with the Pope passing orders down from on high. However, Pope Paul, disappointed with the restiveness of so many within the Church, and especially appalled by the chaotic criticisms of the laity attending the *3rd World Congress of Laity*, which was in session at the same time as the Synod, obviously did not feel that the time was ripe for power-sharing. (There have been *no* more Congresses of the Laity since that time.) The Synod closed in an atmosphere of disappointment. It left Cardinal Wojtyla absolutely committed to the idea of collegiality, convinced that the Papacy must move away from the pyramidal concept and begin to share the decision-making with the rest of the bishops.

The Synod of 1969 was an 'extraordinary' one, especially convened in the wake of widespread criticism (and often outright rejection) of Pope Paul's controversial *Humanae Vitae*, the encyclical on the subject of birth control. (In 1967 the bishops had expressed a hope that no statement would be made on this vexed question, since it was obvious then that any statement would be a conservative one.) The crisis had assumed epic proportions, and while some saw the conflict as a sign of the Church's growing maturity, others feared its imminent collapse.

It was the popularity of the contraceptive Pill, and the growing belief that its use might prove acceptable to the Church, which had caused Pope John XXIII to set up a commission of six to study the matter in 1963. Its brief was limited: to provide some sort of guidance for the Papacy in a situation that was overhung by the threat of a population explosion. But it rapidly became clear that it was time for a radical re-think of the Church's teaching on marriage and birth control. At the end of June 1964, John's successor Pope Paul (having taken all decisions concerning birth control, mixed marriages and clerical celibacy out of the hands of the Council Fathers and reserved them to himself) enlarged the commission to fifty. Experts in moral theology, medicine, demography, canon law, biblical studies, sociology, economics and psychology were called on to give evidence.

At the meeting of the commission in March 1965, it was obvious that a serious doubt existed. Three main tendencies were emerging, one which wanted to uphold the Church's traditional ban on all forms of artificial contraception, one that was prepared to allow the use of the Pill, and a third that would allow other contraceptive measures as well. Cardinal (then Archbishop) Wojtyla, whose book, *Love and Responsibility*, had been translated into French in 1965 and had brought many insights to bear on this troubled question, was appointed to the Fifth Session of the commission which met in April 1966. This was the session which produced a majority report which did not uphold the Church's traditional total ban on all forms of artificial contraception; and a minority report which advocated no change. When in June the sixteen Cardinals and bishops on the commission met to vote on the draft agreement, Cardinal Wojtyla was unaccountably absent. The voting on that occasion was nine in favour of the majority report, three against it and three undecided. (The three who voted against the report were the commission's president, the conservative Cardinal Ottaviani, who was so furious that he had made his own report to the Pope; Bishop Colombo, the Pope's personal theologian; and the Irish Bishop Morris.)

It has never been made clear why Archbishop Wojtyla should have been absent from such a crucial meeting. His traditional views on birth control were known, and it is to be presumed that he would have voted accordingly. But it is suggested that he may have been unwilling to be counted. Dom Alberic Stacpoole OSB who proposed this view in a letter to *The Times* later wrote in the *Catholic Herald*, that Wojtyla was 'a modern man caught in an ancient Church. He would be in favour of *Humanae Vitae*, but it would represent a conflict of duties for him.' (Perhaps it might be more accurate to say that he is a man of tradition who has to live with a contemporary pastoral situation. As a man of integrity, he makes his own choices.)

As the whole world knows, Pope Paul decided to disregard the advice of the experts and the opinion of most of the bishops, and *Humanae Vitae* appeared in July 1968. It re-asserted the Church's traditional teaching on birth control and opened the floodgates of dissent.

(After the appearance of *Humanae Vitae*, Cardinal Wojtyla published a revised edition of *Love and Responsibility* which clarified and stressed his support for the encyclical and which was translated into several languages. But while he supported the encyclical he could also see beyond it. In an article for *Osservatore Romano* he pointed to what he saw as the most important insights of the encyclical, those which saw marriage, as *Gaudium et Spes* had seen it, as 'a communion of persons' and responsible parenthood as an ideal by which that communion is fulfilled. *Humanae Vitae*, he wrote, was concerned to express an anxiety to protect man 'from the danger of altering his most fundamental values'.

The Synod of Bishops convened in 1969 was intended to restore order to the ranks, though before its first meeting there were some fears that the bishops might be spoiling for a fight. As one commentator put it, 'Some people spoke as though the bishops were stealing into Rome with knives beneath their cloaks for a second Ides of March.[2] But unity, however precarious, was saved. The Synod's final declaration was given at the Vatican by Cardinal Karol Wojtyla on October 27th, 1969: 'In our days,' it said, 'during which storms are invading the Church and the world, there is nothing more important than the testimony of union and the spreading of peace. This union in the Church which is desired so ardently by the Christian people depends very largely on the collaboration both between the Supreme Pontiff and the bishops' conferences and between the conferences among themselves.' (issued by Press Dept, U.S. Catholic Conference).

By the time the bishops met again in 1971 the crisis had more or less passed. In that year Cardinal Wojtyla was elected to the Secretariat General of the Synod. Archbishop Worlock who was also a member of the Secretariat suggests that what colleagues valued most in Cardinal Wojtyla was his well-ordered, disciplined mind: 'In debate he was always the last speaker. He would weigh everything up, making notes and numbering his points. Then he'd put up his finger to indicate that he wanted to speak, and he would rather laboriously go through every point and then reach a conclusion which was usually right. He would never be hurried, and we were often kept late because of him. Often he reached the same conclusion as other people had reached a lot earlier and a lot more impetuously, but in his case it was better founded. He has an immense intellect, one of the finest minds I have ever come across.'

1. It is interesting that Britain and Poland, the two countries where democracy was first established, should both have a Bishop/Martyr saint in the early stages of their history.

2. John Harriott in the *Catholic Herald*.

# 13

# These Are Living Stones

CARDINAL WOJTYLA WAS travelling widely by now, in Canada, the USA, Europe, and the Far East. In 1973 he visited Australia, where he was photographed feeding the kangaroos, and New Guinea, where he was shown with a group of feathered tribesmen, and the Philippines. He had already paid several visits to France, Belgium and West Germany and had given conferences in Rome, Milan, Paris and Louvain. (Once while lecturing in Milan he asked the students how many of the Italian Cardinals went ski-ing. When they looked blank, he said, 'In Poland, forty per cent of them do.' And when they looked even more mystified he explained, 'You see, in Poland, Wyszynski counts for sixty per cent.') In subsequent years he was able to visit most of Latin America, and re-visit Canada and the USA. In 1976 he told the Bicentennial Eucharistic Congress in Philadelphia that hardship and persecution had given renewed vigour to the Church in Poland: 'The atheist character of the Government,' he said, 'forces people to affirm their beliefs.' Invited to lecture at Harvard Summer School (in philosophy), he surprised his audience by the sheer force of his ideas; the Director of the Summer School described him afterwards as 'one of the most impressive men I have ever met . . . an absolutely radiant personality.'

He enjoyed travelling, but the consumerism of the capitalist world did not seem to him to be bringing man any closer to happiness than the oppressive Socialism of his own. At a conference in Rome in 1975 (reported in *Oggi*), he spoke of:

> the ever-growing depersonalisation of man. I don't mean only the danger of considering man as a mere instrument of production; I mean the even greater danger that man himself, more or less consciously, is beginning to see himself as a passive element on a production line, subject to any or every kind of manipulation . . .
>
> If contemporary progress . . . is to have a truly human face, then it must seek to provide man not only with the means of obtaining the material necessities of life but also with the opportunities for becoming more human. Unless it can achieve that, progress can only increase the feelings of alienation.

And in the Lenten meditations which he was asked to address to Paul VI and the Curia in 1976 (later published in Italy as *Segno di Contraddizione*), he said:

> Even in liberal regimes, where men are sick with affluence and an overdose of freedom, human life presents a sorry spectacle of abuses and frustrations of every kind. Are these not confirmed by the phenomena of drug addiction, organised terror, and the kidnapping of innocent persons?

The meditations which went to the making of *Segno di Contraddizione* concerned the 'meeting with Christ in the world of today': Wojtyla saw the whole problem of the world today summed up in the words of Simeon when the child Jesus was brought to the Temple in Jerusalem. This child would become, said Simeon, 'a sign of contradiction,' a man who would be rejected. Today, said Wojtyla, Jesus reveals himself as the hope and the light of mankind, but also as a sign which many men reject:

The great poverty of entire nations, particularly in the Third World, the existence of hunger, economic exploitation and colonialism (which is present not only in the Third World) – all this is a rejection of Christ by the powerful, whatever the regime or the cultural tradition. And this kind of rejection of Christ often goes hand in hand with an apparent acceptance of religion, of Christianity, of the Catholic Church, an acceptance of Christ as a recognised element of the nation's culture, its morality and its educational system.

Yes, even where Christ is officially accepted, the real truth of his person, his mission and his gospel is being denied. We are trying to make him fit into our modern consumer programmes. This kind of double-think even among those who claim to follow Christ is a symptom of the times in which we live.[1]

That, he said, was an indirect form of rejection. But other rejections were more open and explicit:

There are countries in which all churches are closed, in which priests are condemned to death for administering the sacrament of Baptism. But for the most part persecution in the second half of the twentieth century is unlike what it was in the past. We live in a world in which everyone proclaims freedom of conscience and religious liberty; in an epoch in which the struggle against religion (which is defined as 'the opium of the people') is carried out discreetly, so that there can be no martyrs. So the programme for today is a persecution that maintains the fiction that there is full religious freedom and that persecution no longer exists. But the facts show clearly that the struggle against religion still exists, and that it is an integral part of the programme. It even seems as though, before man can achieve the earthly paradise, he must first be deprived of the strength he finds in Christ. This strength has been derided as a weakness unworthy of him. Unworthy – or, could it be, inconvenient? For the strong man whose strength derives from his faith in Christ, does not easily allow himself to be pushed into a collective anonymity.[2]

Indeed, the strong man who was also a believer could not be coerced into anonymity, as successive Polish Governments had found out.

At first Mr Gierek genuinely tried to mend his fences with the Church and made many minor concessions. Mr Skarzynski who was responsible for Church affairs boasted that 'as many as twenty permissions' had been granted for the building of churches in 1971.

Fine. Except that the Church was asking for three thousand, and even if the figures were pitched much lower, say at six hundred, they would not get very far at the rate of twenty a year. It is not that the Poles, as some observers have suggested, are addicted to building churches. Churches mean a great deal to them, and they are accustomed to celebrating all their great occasions with a Mass. Massive urbanisation of the country – the towns have more than doubled in the thirty years since the war – means, in Polish terms, the need for many new churches or at least the right to celebrate Mass in school halls. The Government does not give such permission. Existing churches are packed to overflowing: most have eight Masses every Sunday (some have as many as fifteen) and still the people overflow on to the streets. In one new Socialist settlement, where there is no church nor any likelihood of one, Masses are held in a converted flat (eight Masses each Sunday, with about 350 people attending) and in the garden of a private house (twelve Masses with about 500 people).

Building churches continued to be a vexed question. The authorities pleaded shortage of building materials and in any case had other priorities. Incidents multiplied. At the village of Zboza Wielka near Warsaw, the inhabitants took matters into their own hands and built themselves a makeshift chapel. One hundred and fifty policemen arrived to dismantle the structure and remove the consecrated wafers to a church nearby. Cardinal Wyszynski immediately denounced such pointless destruction. 'Unprecedented sacrilege,' he proclaimed angrily, amid threats of arousing his people to a more practical demonstration of their wrath. There was so much fuss that the Government backed down, allowing that a church could be built but insisting that the priest be removed.

Such incidents were commonplace, and even where permission was given, delays and bureaucratic obstruction prevailed. It had taken ten years to win the permission to build the church at Nowa Huta; building began in 1967 but by 1972 it was only half-finished. The people were building it themselves with the aid of funds contributed by organisations from many nations, including the *Sühnezeichen* (Sign of Reconciliation) group in West Germany. The foundation stone had come from St Peter's tomb in Rome, sent by Pope Paul with the following words: 'Take this stone to Poland, and may it be the corner-stone on which a church will stand at Nowa Huta dedicated to the Queen of Poland.' The church was still surrounded by scaffolding, the terrain was covered in rubble, but this did not deter the people of Nowa Huta from holding services there. Sundays and weekdays alike they attended Mass there, standing outside in rain-storm, gale or scorching heat. Once a year Cardinal Wojtyla came there to celebrate Mass for the 400 Poles murdered by the Nazis in the nearby Krzeslawice hills. But bureaucratic obstruction continued, and it would still be another five years before this church was opened.

By 1973 Mr Gierek's good intentions were wearing thin. Two official reports on education stressed the need for a unified educational system which would prepare its recipients for life in a Socialist country. In fact Socialism was to be imposed through the educational system. The school timetable was to be drawn up in such a way as to leave no time for children to receive their optional religious instruction, and very little time for them to be with their families; the number of schools was reduced; and technology replaced the teaching of the humanities. The hierarchy countered that 'such intentions could deny a person his fundamental right to freedom of conscience and religion which are guaranteed in the Polish Constitution. State laws cannot be contrary to the law of God, otherwise they are not binding.'

But the Government stepped up the pressure. In 1975 a document signed by all the bishops denounced the latest hostile moves. 'Some teaching institutes have reached the point where they ask candidates to present a written declaration of atheism.' By this time the harsh realities of life were driving the workers to despair. Poland's economic boom based on foreign credit was over and a looming economic crisis gave rise to more and more shortages and restrictions. Preaching to workers at Nowa Huta, Cardinal Wojtyla underlined other grievances too: 'The Government does not allow you to get promotion because of your beliefs, nor are you allowed to worship in a building.'

Anti-government feeling was running high, and the situation was fraught with anxiety as Cardinal Wojtyla preached a memorable and moving address in Wawel Cathedral on the Feast of the Epiphany 1976 (one of Poland's most popular Feasts. Actually it is one of the greatest feasts of the Orthodox Church. Hence the Greek name which means: the annunciation of Christ to the whole world.)

It is difficult from the point of view of human dignity, from a humanistic point of view, to accept atheism as a political programme. For it is understandable that a man may seek but not find; it is understandable that a man may deny; but it is not understandable that a man may find himself forbidden to believe. If you wish to fill a given office, to reach a given position, you are forbidden to believe. Atheism as the foundation of national life is a painful misunderstanding from the point of view of true human progress. For it is necessary to respect what is in man. This is the first condition of all social life and of all equality between citizens of the same state. . .

We cannot remain silent, these anxieties weigh upon our hearts; the problem is fundamentally one of social ethics. And we, bishops, priests and all believers, cannot be indifferent to the problem. There cannot be a substantial difference between what we are, what we feel we are, and how we are classified and treated. And so it cannot happen that one group of men, one social group – however well-deserving – should impose on the whole people an ideology, an opinion, contrary to the conviction of the majority.

We are all Poland, all of us, believers and unbelievers. But it cannot be that Poland's destiny should be decided by the non-believers against the will of the believers. For Poland is not a chance reality. Poland is a thousand years of history. Poland is this Wawel Castle, this Cathedral, these tombs of our Kings. Poland stands for innumerable victories and innumerable sufferings!

This is all my wish, and the wish is for every man, for every man who believes, for every man who is seeking, that he may seek without the fear that someone may say to him, it is forbidden . . .

My wish is for families, that they may be allowed to bring up their children according to their own Christian convictions. We do not wish to interfere with the families of atheists – that is a matter for themselves and their own consciences . . . But what else can we wish the millions of Christian families in Poland if not to be sure, when they send their children to school, that the school will not impose on them a materialistic view, an atheistic ideology.

The principle of freedom of conscience and of religion must be interpreted to the full. This truth is proclaimed by everyone: from the Second Vatican Council to the

Charter of Human Rights established by the United Nations; and even the Helsinki Conference recognises that it is the inviolable right of the human person. But this inviolable right must be considered to be inviolable. Every condition of social and national life should be arranged in such a way that this right is not violated; so that public life will not create privileges from on high for some – unbelievers – and a second-class status for others – believers. For we are all of us Poland. And we all wish to build our country, because we all love it. Because it is our country, because we are its children. And it is not lawful to treat these huge multitudes of believers as second-rate people just because they are believers.[3]

In June of that year, when it became known that large increases in food prices were to be imposed, violence again broke out. There were riots by factory workers in Radom, Plock and Ursus, and Mr. Gierek faced the possibility of suffering the fate of Mr. Gomulka. A Party HQ in Radom was set on fire. Severe measures were taken against thousands of protesting workers, who were accused of sabotage. Police behaved with extreme brutality, and heavy fines and long prison sentences were handed out – with serious abuses of judicial procedures. Cardinal Wojtyla, who had always maintained close contacts with the workers, expressed himself energetically on the subject of necessary social reform. He encouraged the workers to demand a more just wage and begged the Government to keep prices down and to put an end to the arrests and interrogations. On a more practical level, he encouraged his people to bring financial aid to the families of the oppressed workers.

Mr. Gierek calmly announced (to workers at Mielec) in September that there was no conflict between Church and State and that 'there are areas in which the Church and the State can co-operate fruitfully in the realisation of important national objectives.' As these areas of fruitful co-operation were named as the protection of the family (the Government was alarmed both by the rising divorce rate and the falling birth rate), the fight against alcoholism and 'social indifferentism', represented by absenteeism, the bishops decided to put the record straight. Repeating their request to the Government to stop reprisals against the workers and to reinstate them in their jobs, the bishops agreed with them that the country was in a mess and that everyone ought to pull together: 'Good workmanship is a moral duty and the capacity for self-denial a Christian virtue. However, the conditions for good workmanship and self-denial depend on confidence in the authorities, and that can only be achieved if the authorities show real concern and anxiety about the welfare of all the citizens.' The bishops went on to record further grievances, reminding the Government that the great majority of Polish citizens were practising members of the Catholic Church and that 'the fight against religion is paid for with taxes paid by the practising Catholic.' They complained that building regulations were used to check the progress of religion; that Catholics were discriminated against by being barred from senior appointments and by being ineligible for promotion They condemned the open propaganda for atheism on the media, the misrepresentation of Scripture, the ridiculing of religious observance in the schools and the increase in pornographic literature. (Children from Catholic homes had much greater difficulty in obtaining places in higher education, and therefore it was hard for them to reach even the first rungs of the social ladder.)

They accused the State of seeking to estrange young people from religion. (In schools and universities the young were told that a religious outlook was incompatible with scientific discovery; at holiday camps they were prevented from going to Mass or from wearing medallions; and students were subjected to threats and reprisals to prevent them from attending the university chaplaincies.) The bishops' letter pointed out further that 'one leading State dignitary had disclosed that new dates for school holidays were to be proposed so that they would no longer coincide with the liturgical calendar.'

Some letter. And it exploded Mr Gierek's assertion that relations between Church and State were normal. Although he had frequently asserted that atheism is complex and cannot be simply judged, at the 1977 Synod, Wojtyla had some harsh things to say about atheist attacks on the Church: 'The State favours all the organisations which favour atheism in all its expressions . . . it is programmed atheism . . . the anti-Catechism of the secular world.' The State, said Cardinal Wojtyla, sought 'a type of man who could be subordinated to its own specific ends'.

It was generally conceded that Cardinal Wojtyla's hand could be seen in these outspoken letters from the bishops. He was indeed becoming so outspoken a champion of human rights and freedoms that he was seen as a more dangerous adversary to the regime than the ageing Wyszynski. Unlike the latter he could combat Marxism at the level of theory. Cardinal Wyszynski had been on the scene for so long that nobody could imagine Poland without him, and it is just one of the many paradoxes of Polish life that at about this time he was officially designated a 'Polish patriot'. In this game of diplomatic chess, Wyszynski's moves were predictable; Wojtyla's were not. Although in general he was more conciliatory, Wojtyla was also a more subtle adversary who could get his way by argument and persuasion. A conciliator perhaps, but not a weak man; he was a man of whom to be wary.

The Government's anxiety grew as Wyszynski reached retiring age, and as his health began to give cause for concern. They faced the near-certainty of having Wojtyla as the next Primate, and they did not relish the prospect. Rumour has it that Mr Gierek's Government secretly asked the Vatican if Wyszynski could stay on after retirement age, so that the Primacy of Wojtyla might at least be postponed. Wojtyla was, of course, aware of the rumours, and he let it be known that he had no desire to replace the Primate.

On October 23rd, 1977, Paul VI received the old Cardinal in Rome and re-confirmed him as Primate. But at the same time it was made clear that he should make some attempt to adapt to Paul's policy of better relations with the Communists, and initiate discussions with Mr Gierek.

Five days later there was a truly historic meeting in Warsaw between the Primate and the First Secretary of the Party, a face to face meeting which boded well for the future and led to one extraordinarily positive result. Less than a month after Wyszynski's visit to Rome, Mr Gierek was received by Pope Paul VI in a private audience which lasted one hour and twenty minutes. Afterwards Gierek said of the Pope: 'He is a man whose greatness is recognised by his contemporaries. I am convinced that history will reaffirm this evaluation.' And he expressed a hope that never again would there be a conflict between the Church and the State in Poland. In the same generous vein Paul VI replied: 'The activity of the Catholic Church has always been positive, in the interests of the Polish nation, even outside the specifically religious sector. Today the Church is as willing as ever to offer its own positive contribution to Polish society.'

Another Spring? Or another jerk of the see-saw? In the merry-go-round of Church-State relationships in Poland, nobody could tell. 'The philosophical concepts may be different but the objectives are the same,' commented an official report about the Church, a statement somewhat different in tone from that uttered by a senior official some months earlier: 'If we cannot destroy the Church, at least let us stop it from causing harm.' In Poland one is resigned to such paradoxes.

And perhaps the most significant event of that extraordinary year was the consecration at last of the splendid new church at Nowa Huta, ten years after permission to build had been granted and twenty years after the people were first promised their church. Standing, with poetic irony, at the juncture of Karl Marx and Great Proletarian Avenues (in the older cities the streets are more likely to be called Street of the Holy Cross, of the Holy Spirit or of All the Saints), the Church of Our Lady Queen of Poland has been built to resemble the barque of St Peter, and it flaunts a Cross as high as they could make it. (It could not be higher because of low-flying aircraft.) A plaque near the entrance recalls that the church was built by the people themselves between 1967–77 to celebrate Poland's thousand years of Christianity, and that help was given by 'many nations of good-will'. It makes symbolic reference to the blood and water which flowed from the side of the crucified Christ, when his life blood had drained away. Even now, in 1978, parts of the church are not yet complete, but no one who goes there will ever be able to forget the powerful and dramatic bronze figure of Christ on the Cross which dominates the main body of the building. It bespeaks so much raw suffering that it could only have been sculpted in Poland. Nor can one forget the figures in the crypt – the Pietà, in which Mary holds her child in various attitudes of anguish and supplication, each portrayal representing a different concentration camp. And there too is the figure of Maximilian Kolbe in the striped garb of Auschwitz, a present day symbol of the love that knows no bounds.

Today fifteen Masses are celebrated in the church at Nowa Huta every Sunday, and in addition it is hoped to express something of that love by using the church as a centre for the chronically disabled and the dying.

When he blessed and consecrated that church which in so many ways is symbolic of the spirit of Poland, Cardinal Wojtyla told a weeping but exultant crowd of fifty thousand: 'This city of Nowa Huta was built as a city without God. But the will of God and of the workers here has prevailed. Let us all take the lesson to heart. This is not merely a building,' he added with heartfelt emotion, 'these are living stones.'

1. My own translation from *Segno di Contraddizione*, by kind permission of St Paul Publications whose own *Sign of Contradiction* was not available at the time when this book went to print.

2. Ibid.

3. Reproduced in its entirety in *Osservatore Romano*, 11.3.76.

# 14

# My Friends, Pray For Me . . .

'THERE CANNOT BE many countries in which the champion of the dissident atheist student group is the local Cardinal,' wrote Richard Dowden in the *Catholic Herald*.

And a Marxist student confirms the startling fact:

> I am convinced that everyone, believer and non-believer, will agree that the Church in our country is the only institution that can defend human rights and which fights for genuinely humanitarian relations between the people of our country. For us this stand was inseparably connected with Cardinal Wojtyla who became in a way a symbol of all those trying to retain human dignity.[1]

After the riots of 1976 and the police harassment which followed, a Workers' Defence Committee was set up to ask for the reinstatement of dismissed workers, an unconditional amnesty for those detained and sentenced for their part in the June riots, and the appointment of a Parliamentary Commission 'to conduct an unbiased inquiry into the grave and harrowing problems of the situation'.

No longer was there any division between students and workers. Students all over the country supported the workers' demands and over 1,600 of them petitioned Parliament on their behalf. One of the leading supporters of the Workers' Defence Committee in Cracow was Stanislaw Pyjas, a student in his final year at the Jagiellonian University. On

Saturday May 7th his body was found in the doorway of a block of flats with his head battered in. The authorities maintained that he had fallen down the stairs while under the influence of alcohol, and indeed the autopsy stated that he had drunk the equivalent of half a litre of vodka.[2]

But, to say the least, the death was shrouded in mystery. For one thing the body was found some distance away from the nearest stairs. It was curious that Pyjas had recently been the subject of a vilification campaign: five of his friends had received anonymous letters on April 19th and 20th insinuating that he was a police informer and inciting them to 'settle matters with this nasty character once and for all by any possible means at your command'; and thirdly, Pyjas did not ever touch alcohol.

The Requiem Mass for Pyjas at St Annes University Church was attended by two thousand students who walked in procession after the service to the place where the body had been found. A declaration signed by the Committee for Student Solidarity demanded an inquiry into the death of their friend who had 'died tragically in mysterious circumstances . . .'

> . . . The deceased was a person who held independent and non-conformist views. In the last phase of his life he actively co-operated with the Workers' Defence Council. His death left a deep-felt sense of shock among the academic community, not only in Cracow but throughout the country.[3]

The declaration went on to say that the Cracow students had responded to this mysterious death by deciding to boycott all the events of the annual Rag Week. Cardinal Wojtyla supported and approved this decision and publicly entrusted the students to the care and protection of the citizens of Cracow. This did not prevent either students or citizens being harassed by the police, however. Many who went to pay their respects at the site of Pyjas's death were detained and arrested and the place itself was desecrated. But Wojtyla's support for the students won him this praise from a dissident atheist student:

When in May 1977 after the murder (sic) of our friend there were demonstrations in Cracow and members of the Workers' Defence Committee were imprisoned, there was a strong possibility that all of us would share their fate and find ourselves in prison. It was therefore all the more important that Cardinal Wojtyla spoke out and entrusted the students to the care of the town. He is the representative of a Church which for years has not been in authority. It is a fighting and struggling Church, a symbol, a sign for the whole world.[4]

Among many of the students there was a great spiritual hunger of which Wojtyla was well aware. In the Lenten talks he had given at the Vatican the previous year he had referred to similar talks and spiritual Retreats being given all over Poland – many of them for the young at their own request. In the Cracow archdiocese provision had been made for two thousand places for students in their last high school year, but applications came from nearly twice that number. And it had been the same in the summer.

I often talked to those young people and listened with close attention to their experiences . . . for them these spiritual exercises are first and foremost a way of encountering God, of discovering both God and themselves in the realisation that their lives have a purpose. Those youngsters often come from a great darkness, a darkness to which they are condemned by the secularising and anti-religious system of official education. Yet from out of this darkness those young people are walking trustfully into the presence of God, learning to trust in the ultimate sense and purpose of their world.[5]

But it was not only the Church which complained that young people were being brought up on an unwholesome intellectual diet. By this time many left-wing groups had become thoroughly disenchanted with the education being offered in schools and universities. Philosophy, history and literature all received a one-sided Marxist slant, and top priority was given to not offending the Soviet Union. 'Why, for example,' asked one graduate, 'do the history books make no reference to the nineteenth-century Russian occupation of our country, or even the Ribbentrop-Molotov Pact in 1939?' Polish culture was being distorted and impoverished by such propagandist omissions.

Hence the revival of the Flying University. 'The Flying University', says an elderly Pole succinctly, 'teaches things the Government would prefer it not to.'

In 1977 a group of dissident intellectuals decided to make good the deficiencies of the schools and universities and start their own lecture courses. They set up the Society for Academic Courses, the official name for what everybody knows as the Flying University – the traditional Polish answer to attempts to stamp out its culture. But this time there was a difference; this time the group of intellectuals refused to go underground, refused to be clandestine. It was unofficial, it was frowned upon, but it was not illegal and it proudly (and bravely) proclaimed its existence and the names of its lecturers.

Determined to combat the partial truths and deliberate omissions dear to the official education system, the Society organised several series of lecture courses on literature, history, philosophy and the social sciences. Lectures were usually given in private homes and in village halls, and they were attended sometimes by twenty or thirty, sometimes by one hundred and fifty or even more. (In fact, in Wroclaw Cathedral on October 22nd, 1978, 1,200 students gathered to hear Professor Bartoszewski's lecture on 'The Individual in a Totalitarian System'.) News of lectures was passed by word of mouth or over foreign radio stations, or even openly on photographed sheets passed round in the universities. (Access to xerox is under strict control.) The titles were not such as to fire the imagination, 'Society and Pedagogy', 'Social and Political Ideology from the French Revolution to the Second World War', 'Literature as an expression of social consciousness'.[6] Those who attended them were in search not of entertainment but of truth, and in attending they put themselves at risk.

The police did not like the new development and both lecturers and students often found themselves in prison on a forty-eight-hour arrest. (They usually prepared for this eventuality by tape-recording the lectures in advance.) The people in whose homes the lectures took place were particularly vulnerable to police swoops, but 'temporary arrests' were often made at railway stations.

It says much for the gradual growth of understanding between the Church and the dissident Marxists that the bishops did not hesitate to offer their support. (A correspondent from Poland wrote recently in the *Tablet*: 'There has been considerable discussion of possible dialogue between the Church and the 'left opposition' . . . But dialogue at a meaningful philosophical level is by no means fully established yet, and the response from certain churchmen has been somewhat cautious . . . Extensive dialogue still remains somewhat a desideratum for the future, *though one to which both sides attach considerable importance*.'[7] (The italics are mine.)

Expressing their disapproval of 'all actions which hinder the human spirit from creating free cultural values', the bishops proceeded to pledge their support to 'those initiatives which aim at presenting culture, the works of the spirit and the history of the nation in an authentic form, for the nation has a right to the objective truth about itself.'[8]

Everyone knew to which 'initiatives' the bishops were referring. In Cracow Cardinal Wojtyla declared that the Church's mission was not concerned only with moral theology but with enabling men and women to develop as human beings and to become responsible members of a free society. 'And if society is so constituted as to prevent them from achieving their potential, then the Church must step in.'

Wojtyla supported the students' stand: 'Everyone should be given the right to express his own views,' he said, 'and it is useless to try to force young people into a uniform mould.'

It was difficult at first to find ways in which the Church could make its contribution to the Flying University's programme. Lectures could hardly be inserted into ordinary after-school catechism lessons or into public sermons. After much thought Wojtyla offered the use of five Cracow churches in which lectures could be given. (Householders on whose premises lectures were given could be fined as much as a month's salary on the grounds that the over-crowding contravened safety and health regulations, but there was no such excuse if the meetings were held in a church.)

The gesture was one of the Cardinal's last in Cracow – and it was notable that among those who were refused visas to attend the installation ceremony in Rome were three of his personal friends: Mr Jacek Wózniakowski, a publisher, Mr Tadeusz Mazowiecki, editor of the Catholic philosophical monthly, *Wiez*, and Mr Bohdan Cywinski, editor of *Znak*, a well-known author, and a participant, together with the other two, in the hunger-strike which took place in St Martin's Church, Warsaw from May 20th–27th, 1977 in protest against the Government's harsh treatment of the workers. All three men are lecturers in the Flying University. Nobody was really surprised to learn, when the second academic year opened in November 1978, that many of the courses had been postponed because the lecturers had been arrested. The following appeared in the Catholic Herald of November 24th:

A priest in Poland was interrogated and intimidated by state officials last week after giving a lecture on Polish tradition to about 150 students of the so-called Flying University.

The incident came only a few weeks after a Catholic trade unionist was allegedly beaten up by police. The man was later sentenced to two months detention, and charged with assault. If found guilty he faces up to eight years in prison . . .

\*     \*     \*

The Flying University will have lost a champion now that Cardinal Wojtyla has gone; and the people of Cracow also. 'He is a truly great man,' said one of the leaders of the Catholic Intelligentsia Clubs, 'the only man I have ever met whose authority I would accept without questioning. He never thought of himself, he served people, listened to them and looked to their best interests. He is the best man that we had in Poland.'

And a girl student recalled a poignant memory: 'I remember one occasion when we shared bread, I remember saying to Cardinal Wojtyla that I hoped the Polish bishops would not be disappointed in the young people of Poland. The Cardinal's reply moved me deeply: he said that *his* hope was that the young people of Poland would not be disappointed in their bishops!'

In Wojtyla they were not disappointed.

\*     \*     \*

On August 6th 1978 Pope Paul VI died.

Cardinal Wojtyla went to the Franciscan monastery of Kalwaria to say Mass for him. He loved Kalwaria, which is near Cracow but nearer still to his birthplace of Wadowice; he loved the huge baroque church with its onion towers, overlooking the valley from a hilltop. Frequently he took groups of pilgrims there to make the Way of the Cross over its six kilometres of paths and its forty-two wayside shrines, wearing gumboots and sharing an umbrella when it rained, holding a rosary in one hand and a ski stick in the other when the snow and ice lay on the ground. For many years Kalwaria had been a refuge in good times and bad: on arrival he would put down his suitcase and set off on a thirty kilometre walk – to Markow and back, a round trip of eight hours which invigorated him.

But on this visit he remained in the church lost in prayer, and the monks saw that he looked strained and worried.

After Kalwaria, he left for Rome and for the Conclave of Cardinals which elected sixty-five-year-old Cardinal Albino Luciani as Pope John Paul I after only eight hours of deliberation. It was a surprising but popular choice, and the new Pope's smile won him the admiration and affection of the world; everyone seemed suddenly aware of the Papacy, as they had not been since the death of 'Good Pope John'. Pope John Paul, it appeared, had been elected for his ability to get on with people, to open windows that had been too long closed. He was not, as Popes so often were, a Vatican diplomat, but a pastor, gentle, kind, humorous, profoundly spiritual, genuinely humble. John Paul, rejecting the use of the papal tiara and the whole triumphalism of the coronation ceremony, was installed at a modest ceremony (by Vatican standards anyway) on September 3rd.

When Wojtyla returned from Rome the look of strain had gone from his face, and he seemed relaxed and cheerful again. (Six weeks later after he had been made Pope himself, a friend of his, a respected academic, said: 'A few of us had long been convinced that one day he would be Pope. It was a genuine conviction, not a romantic hope. When Paul VI died and Wojtyla went to Rome, we believed that the time had come and we braced ourselves to say goodbye to him. I myself was amazed when somebody else was elected, so strong was my belief that it would be Wojtyla.')

But for the moment there was relief, and Cardinal Wojtyla went out to Kalwaria where he said a Mass of Thanksgiving and invited a large crowd from all over the archdiocese to join him in prayers for the new Pope.

On Sunday, September 17th a 'pastoral letter' from the Polish bishops was read in the churches – a letter which was said to have been strongly influenced by Wojtyla. It was an appeal to the Government to allow the Church access to the mass media – the Church's only mouthpiece is the Catholic Press, and that is both heavily restricted and censored. The Church is banned from the national press, radio and television. The bishops' letter is worth quoting:

All of (the mass media) are the property of the whole human family. Everybody has a right to use them . . . The Church through the use of the media wants to popularise religious and spiritual values and thereby strengthen the unity of all men.

Alas, the Church in Poland today, even though it has been co-operating with national culture since the beginnings of the existence of the State, nevertheless has not only been refused the right to possess the mass communications media, in particular radio, television and the daily press, but also has been prevented from actively using them. All the media have been taken over by the State and made to serve the ideology which aims at bringing up human beings without God . . .

Things are not as they should be. The mass communications media are abused in order to impose one kind of view only and one behaviour pattern only, and to exert power over people . . .

To ignore our opinion, the opinion of the consumers, is to treat us as objects to be manipulated at will by those who have acquired power over the citizens, the citizens who have been deprived of the right to pronounce their views publicly.

Referring perhaps to the Church's increasing share in the Flying University, the letter continued:

In order to be able to assume an active posture vis-à-vis the (media), we must take on the toil and duty of self-education, so that the pressure exerted now by these media may not blunt or even destroy in us the capacity for critical assessment . . . We all know that the spirit of freedom is the proper climate for the full development of a person. Without freedom a person is stunted and all progress halts. Not to allow people with a different social and political ideology to speak, as is the practice of the State, is unjust. State censorship has always been and remains a weapon of totalitarian systems. With the aid of censorship the aim is not only to influence the mental life of society and public opinion but even to paralyse the cultural and religious life of the whole people. Social life requires frankness and freedom of opinion. Censorship places blinkers over the eyes of our people . . . it misinforms them and – even worse – releases them from their responsibility for their nation.

After pointing out the great shortage of Catholic periodicals in a nation of believers, seventy-five per cent of whom are practising Catholics – the total edition of the three Catholic weeklies amounted only to 190,000, while the demand for these is in millions – the bishops asked specifically that at least a Sunday Mass might be broadcast 'for those who are ill and suffering'. And it concluded: 'We have the right to expect the voice of millions of believing citizens of our country to be heard.'[9]

Cardinal Karol Wojtyla signed the document, the last he would ever sign as Cardinal of Cracow. And there is a considerable irony in the fact that the embargo on the broadcasting of religious services in Poland would first be broken when his own inauguration as Pope was broadcast live from Rome.

On September 28th he celebrated his twentieth anniversary as a bishop by saying Mass in Wawel Cathedral at the altar where Pope John XXIII had once said Mass as a young priest in 1912. It was an altar with a special Polish significance too, Queen Jadwiga's altar, where reputedly she once held a conversation with Christ.

After only thirty-three days, Pope John Paul died. He had shown no sign of exhaustion on the previous evening, and had visited the chapel for night prayers as usual. Before he retired his staff had told him of a shooting in Rome, the killing of a Communist youth by a group of right-wing extremists. 'Ah,' sighed the Pope, 'they are all killing each other, even the young.' Those were the last words anyone heard him speak. Next morning, after he had failed to appear at Mass, one of his secretaries went to his room and found him dead, in bed, with his reading lamp still on and a copy of the *Imitation of Christ* open beside him. The papal physician was summoned and declared that he had died of a massive stroke.

Cardinal Wojtyla went to Kalwaria one last time, said Mass before the altar dedicated to Maximilian Kolbe, and prayed fervently that the Cardinals would make a wise choice.

'My friends, pray for me,' he said urgently as he left for Rome, never to return as the Cardinal Archbishop of Cracow.

1. Everyman film, *How Is It In Cracow?* BBC 2, 22.10.78.
2. *Dissent in Poland 1976–77*. Reports and Documents in translation, produced by the Association of Polish Students and Graduates in Exile.
3. Ibid.
4. Everyman film, *How Is It In Cracow?* BBC 2, 22.10.78.
5. *Segno di Contraddizione*. See Acknowledgments.
6. 'Polish Academe', *The Tablet*, 25.11.78.
7. Ibid.
8. Ibid.
9. With acknowledgements to Keston College, the centre for the study of Religion and of Communism.

# 15

# It's Cold up There
# On The Mountain . . .

JUST OVER A thousand years ago, Mieszko I, first king of
Poland, went on pilgrimage to Rome 'to make a gift of
Poland' to the throne of St Peter. Cardinal Karol Wojtyla
did not know that history was about to repeat itself as he
journeyed to Rome for the funeral of John Paul I and for
the Conclave which would elect his successor.

At Fiumicino airport he joked with a posse of newsmen
who rushed to photograph him. 'Don't waste your time,' he
laughed. 'You don't imagine they're going to make *me*
Pope, do you?' A year earlier he had been asked on Italian
television about the prospects of a Polish Pope being
elected (the interviewer probably had Cardinal Wyszynski
in mind). 'No,' he had answered, shaking his head. 'The
time is not yet ripe.'

*Morto un papa, se ne fa un' altro*', goes a Roman saying, –
'when a Pope dies, another one takes his place.' One
hundred and eleven Cardinals were arriving in Rome to
elect a successor for the man they had chosen only a few
weeks before. Depressed by John Paul's sudden death, and
worried that they had placed him under an intolerable
strain, they recognised the need to find a man who was
physically strong as well as *papabile* in other respects. The
choice of a younger man could not be ruled out.

Contrary to popular belief, the election of a Pope bears
no resemblance to a political election. Most of the important work is done beforehand, as the Cardinals meet, dis-

cuss and learn more about each other, each one knowing that like everyone else he is under a microscope. This time there were no certainties, except perhaps that the next man like all the others would be Italian. Yet even that was not beyond doubt – had not Pope John Paul I said before the last Conclave that he thought the time had come for a Third World Pope? He himself had consistently favoured the election of Cardinal Lorscheider of Argentina, an outspoken advocate of social justice.

At the August election a number of Cardinals had been front-runners, and each of these had had a strong chance of being elected. But in the space of thirty-three days everything had changed. The candidates who had formerly been considered *papabile* (having the necessary qualities for a Pope) – Pironio, Baggio, Pignedoli, Lorscheider and others – already belonged to the past and somehow were *hors de concours*. John Paul's brief term had introduced a new pastoral style to the Papacy; (it *was* a question of style, since there had been no time for achievements;) he had breathed warmth and life into dry bones, and had opened the door to a new evangelical simplicity. He had shown that in a world accustomed to swift means of communicating it is necessary to be a communicator. The radiant and natural smile of the old man from Venice was an instant asset: 'He put an end to the sad face of the Papacy. His meteoric pontificate suddenly made all things possible.'[1]

Quite obviously a Pope cannot be chosen for his smile, nor can a smile be manufactured. But the lesson was clear: the new Pope must possess the ability to draw people to himself (if it were not such an overworked word, one would say he had to have charisma); and he must be in good health.

The Italian Catholic Press wanted Cardinal Siri of Genoa, a man who had been described as 'the arch-conservatives' conservative' and who had said of Pope John's Council that it would take the Church fifty years to recover from it. Cardinal Siri, who had been considered *papabile* at the 1958 election which produced Pope John, was the candidate of all those in the Church who wanted to turn the clocks back and forget that the Council had ever happened. The favourite of the less reactionary Italians was Cardinal Giovanni Benelli who, as Paul's assistant Secretary of State was said to have virtually ruled in the Vatican and who had made very many enemies inside the Curia.

As the election drew near most of the world's press were speculating about the chances of these two, although other names were mentioned, among whom was Cardinal Basil Hume of London. Then Cardinal Siri over-reached himself. He had been unwise enough to give an interview to a Turin newspaper, *Gazzetta del Popolo*, in the course of which he had been asked his views about collegiality. 'Collegiality?' he had snapped, 'I haven't the faintest idea what it is.' This article was embargoed until October 15th by which time all the Cardinals should have been safely inside the Sistine Chapel; but unluckily for Cardinal Siri the embargo was overlooked (the interviewer was said to be a friend of Cardinal Benelli) and the article, appearing on Saturday the 14th, effectively scuppered his chances. The *coup de grace* quite possibly came from Cardinal König of Vienna. Asked if Cardinal Siri would restore the triumphalist coronation ceremony if he were to be elected, König replied: 'No, he would have a simple humble ceremony in St Peter's Square; but then afterwards in private he would have a marvellous coronation with all his friends present and incense billowing all over the place.'[2]

Such unseemly politicking among the Italians probably did much to rule them out of court. 'As it turned out,' says Father F. X. Murphy, a renowned Vaticanologist, 'their acrimonious rivalry secured the election of a non-Italian Pope.' Yet when on the afternoon of Saturday October 14th the Cardinals disappeared behind the high walls of the Vatican, very few doubted that an Italian would be elected.

As the Cardinals began their deliberations beneath the huge frescoes of Michelangelo, they were fully conscious of the weight of responsibility now theirs, and their general air was one of pessimism. A few hours before entering the Chapel, Cardinal Ursi of Naples had voiced what was probably a general feeling: 'Whoever becomes Pope,' he said, 'will have much to suffer. It will be in his reign that we shall see the decisive battle between materialism and Christian humanism.'

With no thoughts of becoming Pope, Cardinal Wojtyla's last act before going inside was to ring a friend and ask him to book him on to the first possible flight back to Cracow. He took with him into the Conclave a small volume of Marxist theory! 'Isn't that heretical?' someone asked. 'Oh, I think I'm quite safe,' he countered.

No one can know for certain how the voting went, for the simple reason that the Cardinals are forbidden, on pain of excommunication, to reveal what happened. However, given the hints that abound, it is usually possible for skilled Vatican-watchers to work out the probabilities. According to a usually reliable source, *Informations Catholiques Internationales*,[3] this then is an account of the two days which followed:

*Sunday October 15th*

In the lead after the first ballot were Cardinals Benelli, Siri and Felici, each one with about thirty votes, with the first two having slightly more than thirty and Felici slightly less. Other votes were scattered among other Italians and a few 'foreigners', among them Wojtyla who is said to have gained some votes at the August Conclave at this same stage.

On the second ballot many of the votes previously cast for Felici now went to Benelli who, many people say, came near to getting the necessary two-thirds majority. The supporters of Cardinal Siri, however, had no intention of seeing Benelli elected and though in the third ballot he was still in the lead, by the fourth he had lost ground, thanks to the blocking tactics of the Siri group. There was a sprinkling of other candidates, Colombo of Milan, Ursi of Naples, and an increasing number of votes for non-Italians, among them Wojtyla. By the end of that day, when the second lot of black smoke was seen by the disappointed crowd in St Peter's Square, the Cardinals knew they had passed the point of no return and were looking for a non-Italian Pope.

That evening more discussions and conversations took place, and Cardinal König emerged as the most likely candidate.

### Monday October 16th

Next morning there were two ballots whose outcome is far from clear. At lunch that day Cardinal König let it be known that he would not accept the election and suggested that the votes which might have been cast for him should go instead to his friend the Archbishop of Cracow who had always been noted for his commitment to the reforms of Vatican II. The other Germans and Cardinal Jubany of Barcelona also pressed for support for Wojtyla, and the idea seemed to appeal to at least one of Cardinal Siri's former supporters, the Polish-American Cardinal Krol of Philadelphia. (Other sources have reported that at this lunch a Cardinal who raised his glass across the table in friendly greeting to Cardinal Wojtyla received a very unhappy look in exchange.)

The last ballot (and nobody is sure whether it was the seventh or the eighth) was conclusive: Cardinal Karol Wojtyla was asked whether he would accept the Papacy.

Newspapers and journals have reported that he paused for so long that the Cardinals were afraid that he was going to refuse. But Cardinal Sin of Manila has told what really took place. When Wojtyla was asked 'Do you accept?' he slowly brought out Pope Paul VI's *Constitution on the Election of a Pope* and read aloud the following:

We ask him who is elected not to refuse the office to which he has been elected for fear of its weight, but to submit himself humbly to the Divine Will; for God Who imposes the burden sustains him with His hand lest he be unequal to bearing it; in conferring the heavy task upon him, God also helps him to accomplish it and, in giving him the dignity, he grants him also the strength, lest in his weakness he should fall beneath the weight of his office.

He put down the document and paused for a moment before continuing:

I come from a Church which has suffered much for the faith and I have been part of that suffering. Now *you* are asking me to accept even greater suffering as Supreme Pastor of that Church.

In the pause that followed, the Cardinals held their breath. Even now they thought he might refuse. Then: 'I accept,' he said, adding, 'Because of my reverence, love and devotion to John Paul and also to Paul VI who was my inspiration and my strength, I shall take the name of John Paul.'

Whereupon the indomitable old warrior Wyszynski came to him and embraced him, and the two Poles stood there 'for a full three minutes', with tears streaming down their cheeks. The emotional atmosphere was so highly charged that many of the Cardinals felt oppressed by it.

Then applause broke out in the Sistine Chapel.

\*    \*    \*

Most of the rest is now history except for one small but not insignificant exchange between the new Pope and Mgr Noè, the Curial Master of Ceremonies: 'Your Holiness will now go out on to the balcony and give the Blessing,' said Noè.

'And I shall speak to the people,' said John Paul II.

'But, Your Holiness, that is not normal procedure,' said Noè.

'I shall speak to the people,' said John Paul II.

\*     \*     \*

Later that evening a still emotional Cardinal Wyszynski broadcast a message on Vatican Radio, saying:

> I embrace you, my brother, companion of my toil and of the struggle for the Church in our country. Rejoice, Poland, for you have been asked to give the finest of your sons, one who has grown to maturity amid the trials and the sufferings of our nation.

So the Roman Catholic Church had elected the 264th successor to St Peter, the youngest Pope since Pio Nono, who had been elected in 1846 at the age of fifty-four, the first non-Italian for over four and a half centuries and the first Pope from behind the so-called Iron Curtain, the whole of whose priestly experience had been acquired under a Communist regime. The last non-Italian was the unlucky Dutchman, Hadrian VI, whose featureless one-year reign, was remarkable only because it led to an Italian monopoly of the Holy See.

Once the choice had been made, it seemed to be both surprising yet utterly right. The Cardinals appeared to be as surprised as anyone. 'We go from one surprise to another, thanks to the Holy Spirit,' confided Cardinal Marty of Paris to a friend. 'I'm absolutely delighted,' smiled a Cardinal from Brazil. 'It's as if a Third World candidate had won.'

Not unexpectedly, though, some of the Italians were bitterly disappointed. An American magazine quoted one Curial prelate as saying: 'If the last Conclave gave a flunking grade to the Curia, this one extended it to the whole Italian hierarchy.'[4] And when Cardinal Siri was asked what he thought of the Pope's first speech from the balcony, he replied sourly, as he got into his car, 'I don't know. I can't remember what he said.'

\*       \*       \*

On the following morning, speaking in Latin, Pope John Paul delineated a charter for the Roman Catholic Church, pledging himself to follow the decrees of the Vatican Council and to take up the challenge of 'that Magna Carta of the Council, the Dogmatic Constitution, *Lumen Gentium*'. He made it quite clear that the Council documents were not mere pieces of paper but growth points to be developed and deepened; and though he stressed the primacy of Peter he was at pains to refer five times to collegiality in the course of his speech. (By the time he had finished, Cardinal Siri must have known what it was.) Those who were anxious to hear his views on ecumenism breathed more freely when he said:

> We cannot forget our brothers of other churches and Christian confessions. The ecumenical cause is actually so important and so delicate that we cannot refrain from referring to it. How many times have we meditated together on the last wish of Christ that asks the Father for the gift of unity for his disciples. And who does not recall the insistence of St Paul on 'the communion of the spirit' which leads one to be united in love with a common purpose and a common mind in the imitation of Christ our Lord? It does not seem possible that there will still remain the drama of the division between Christians – a cause of confusion and perhaps even of scandal.
>
> We intend therefore to proceed along the way already begun, by encouraging those steps which serve to remove obstacles. Hopefully then, thanks to a common effort, we might arrive finally at a full communion.

John Paul stressed his desire for peace and international

justice, but stressed equally that 'we have no intention of political interference'. He made no pretence that the way ahead was straight or even clear, and he could make no easy promises:

> Brothers, dear sons and daughters, the recent happenings in the Church and in the world, are for all of us a healthy warning: What will our Pontificate be like? What fate has the Lord in store for his Church in the years to come? What road will humanity take as it approaches the year 2000? These are crucial questions. But the only answer to them is 'God knows.'

It was clear that he would be open to whatever the future might hold. And when later that day he reminded the Cardinals that the scarlet of their robes symbolised a faithfulness 'even to the shedding of blood', it was also clear that he had no illusions about the task that lay ahead.

\*      \*      \*

Since his election, John Paul must have given nightmares to the Vatican officials, so long the slaves of protocol. He would have none of it; nor did he intend to be, as previous Popes had been, 'a prisoner of the Vatican'. A man who had shown himself adept at dealing with the local Party was not likely to be scared of the bureaucrats in the Curia.

So on the first Tuesday afternoon, after finishing his speech 'to the Church and the World', he set off to visit an old friend and colleague, Bishop Andrzej Deskur who was very ill in a Rome clinic. The stunned Vatican officials tried to dissuade him but in vain. When he emerged from the clinic he made some remarks to the crowd, but he forgot that they might expect a blessing. An escorting prelate duly reminded him and John Paul turned and blessed the crowd, afterwards saying cheerfully, 'You see, even a Pope has to learn his trade.' Two weeks later he went again to see

Bishop Deskur, this time dressed in a plain black cassock and accompanied only by a secretary and two security guards.

This break with hidebound tradition prompted a Rome critic to remark that soon the Holy Father would be careering round Rome on a motor-cycle. 'Nonsense,' snorted a friend in Cracow, 'he couldn't manage anything more mechanised than a bicycle.'

There was delighted gossip that he had baulked at the food provided in the Vatican and had installed a Polish nun in the kitchen to fry ham and sausage for his breakfast; had done away with the afternoon siesta; exercised every morning at five am on the roof-terrace built by Paul VI; was having the Vatican tennis court made fit for use (Paul VI had turned it into a helicopter pad), and had replaced the fine Italian wines at table by beer. ('If the Italians had realised his taste in wines,' murmured a Polish friend, 'they'd have thought twice about electing him.')

But the real shock of that first week came at the Press reception for two thousand journalists in the Hall of Benedictions. The Vatican has always been noted for a certain circumspection, not to say deviousness, in its dealings with the Press. As one Catholic editor put it: 'Official information from the Vatican Press Office must make Kremlin spokesmen seem like chatty salesmen.'[5] At a stroke all that was changed. After listening to an introductory Curial address full of unctuous formality, John Paul made his own speech, addressing his audience in French, and while he reminded them of their professional responsibilities, he also reminded the Vatican Press Office of its own, expressing the hope that 'those seeking information about the Church should always be able to find all the help they need. (Press officers) should welcome such inquiries, respecting their convictions and their profession, and provide them with full and objective documentation, explaining at the same time the Christian perspective which gives the facts their true significance for the Church and for humanity.'[6]

Having delivered his speech, using 'I' instead of 'we' throughout, he cupped his hands and announced that he would give the journalists a blessing. Then, to the horror of his aides, John Paul began a slow progress through the Hall of Benedictions, pausing to talk with this one or that, joking with journalists, chatting with nuns, answering any questions they cared to ask. Reporters who remembered the days of taking dictation from Pius XII on bended knee thought they were dreaming. He refused to be hustled and it took him forty-seven minutes to get from one end of the Hall to the other. The journalists seized the opportunity. Would he, they asked, give a full Press conference. 'When they let me,' the Pope replied. It was in any case, as the *Tablet* commented, 'the first Papal press conference in history,' and '*they*' could not have taken much comfort from his remark.

If the Press reception showed the Pope's imaginative flair and passion for free speech, his passion for freedom of belief was equally evident on the Sunday afternoon when, after the ordeal of the installation, he met the heads of the non-Roman Catholic Churches in his study. There were about fifty or sixty in all, including representatives of the Orthodox and Oriental Churches and a strong Anglican contingent from Britain. Pope John Paul greeted each of them with a firm kiss on both cheeks and emphasised again that there was no going back on ecumenism: 'It is not a matter of choice but the wish and prayer of Christ.' Then with the superb sense of theatre which is so obviously integral to his nature, he asked them to join hands in two concentric circles of prayer. 'Let's all hold hands,' he suggested. It was a dramatic gesture which took the breath away. 'One half-expected cracks to appear in the Papal study,' commented a journalist.'[7] Dr Donald Coggan, the first Archbishop of Canterbury ever to attend a Papal installation, said afterwards: 'He is a warm man, a man of love; he goes out to meet you and doesn't wait for you to come to him. He is also a man of courage, a strong man.

And I think he is a joyful man; his face in repose at a service is perhaps rather a sad face, but when he smiles the sun comes out. Warm, strong and joyful – it seems to me that anybody who possesses those three characteristics possesses the essential hallmarks of Christianity.'

There remained only the official delegations, among them the Polish Head of State, Mr Jablonski. Speaking to the assembled delegations, John Paul made a plea for unity and co-operation which would not be lost on the listening Poles:

> There cannot be real human progress, without a courageous, loyal and unselfish search for co-operation and unity among all people.

Mr Jablonski and Mr Kakol stayed behind and were received in private audience. What was said is not known, though one topic is almost certain. Next May will see the celebrations in Cracow Cathedral for the 900th anniversary of the death of St Stanislaus. It is unthinkable that Pope John Paul should not be invited to attend. Or is it? The headache for the Polish Government must be considerable, and like it or not John Paul must abide by their decision.

A realisation of the freedom he had lost must have come home to him forcibly when a week later he was flown in an Italian Air Force helicopter to the hilltop monastery of Mentorella, west of Rome. As Cardinal, he had loved to go there, climbing the last eight miles to the monastery, tasting the freedom of the hills, savouring the companionship of the Polish monks who lived there. Invariably he stayed the night and roamed the hills again next day. He had gone to Mentorella to pray 'for a wise choice' immediately before the Conclave which had elected him Pope. On this visit he spent ninety minutes in prayer before an eleventh-century wooden statue of the Virgin, and then strode out to meet the crowds of pilgrims who had gathered to greet him. He blessed the sick, hugged the children and shook hands with all around him. He threw the children up in the air and caught them, smothering them in a bear hug. There were cries not of *Viva il Papa* but of the far less formal *Viva il papa Wojtyla*. Then the helicopter rushed him back to the Vatican before dusk, while police and carabinieri mounted guard along the route below.

'It is a heavy and terrifying burden they have placed on his shoulders,' wrote Tadeusz Zychiewicz in *Tygodnik Powszechny*. 'It is cold up there on the mountain. With all our hearts we wish him the strength to bear the cold, knowing as we do that he will not only be cold but alone. May God be always near him.'

1. Richard Dowden in the *Catholic Herald*, 27.10.78.
2. Quoted by Peter Hebblethwaite in *Year of Three Popes*.
3. No. 532, November 1978.
4. *Newsweek*, 30.10.78.
5. Richard Dowden in the *Catholic Herald*.
6. *Informations Catholiques Internationales* No. 532, November 1978.
7. 'A Day To Remember', *The Tablet*, 28.10.78.

# 16

# Pope For The World

'WILL HE BE like "il papa Luciani"?' an Italian journalist asked an old friend of the Pope's. 'No,' came the reply, 'he will be like no one but "il papa Wojtyla".'

Pope John Paul II will have his own style, and we already have some idea of what that style will be: he will be open, friendly, accessible, not standing on ceremony.

But what are the questions which overhang the election of this Polish Pope? The first one arises from precisely the fact that he comes from Poland. The Cardinals were all anxious to stress that this was not a political appointment, that the fact of Wojtyla's provenance from behind the Iron Curtain was the merest accident; he was the best man there was, and everything else about him was just a bonus. 'Had Cardinal Wojtyla been an Italian, a Frenchman or even an Englishman, he'd still have been elected,' averred Cardinal Hume of Westminster. The advantages of his Polishness possibly outweigh the disadvantages. Taking a narrow viewpoint, his election should strengthen the Catholic Church in Poland, where it is at least possible that the Communist authorities will be reasonably amenable. Also the oppressed Christians (not only Roman Catholics) of the countries of Eastern Europe will see this election as a sign of the Churchs concern for them, and will accordingly feel more confident of their future.

But how advantageous will this be? How are the Communist governments in those countries going to act? If the

Christians get restive and try their strength, what measures will they take? Will John Paul negotiate with the governments of Lithuania, the Ukraine, Romania, Latvia, Czechoslovakia, Hungary? Or will he, as he said in his election address, steer clear of political interference, and content himself with good advice and moral support to the Christians in those countries?

The Russians cannot be expected to like (and they do *not* like) the presence of a Polish Pope on the world scene. 'I would say that we view the election as destabilising,' commented one Soviet official. In the event of a crunch it will be their moves which count, not those of John Paul. Will he perhaps seek to improve relations with the Soviet Union, and will that inevitably be at the expense of smaller, oppressed countries? And, biggest imponderable in this sea of imponderables, what happens in Russia when Brezhnev dies and a new regime takes over?

Again, it has been objected that the new Pope knows only the Polish situation and will see the world in Polish terms; his Church is a *Volkskirche* governed by extraordinary circumstances such as prevail nowhere else. There are a number of half- or quarter-truths in that contention, but they are certainly not the whole truth. In the first place he has travelled widely in Italy, France, Germany, the USA, Canada, Australia, New Zealand, the Philippines, and his work as a member of four permanent Vatican Congregations, on the Council for the Laity and on the General Secretariat of the Synod has brought him into contact with ideas and people from all over the world. Secondly this narrow Polish Church is one of the few Churches in the world which has young people queuing up to enter its seminaries, and it has priests and more to spare; it is not generally known that last year (1977) the Poles sent fifty-four missionary priests to join the thousands of others working in many different countries. And thirdly, that Polish experience may be immensely valuable in itself: it has equipped Wojtyla admirably for the inevitable and necessary Catholic-Marxist dialogue, since, although his anti-Communist credentials are impeccable, he has also known how to live with Marxism and is prepared to co-operate on equal terms with Marxists. He is well aware, because he is familiar with the Marxist ideology both in theory and in practice, that the issues are complex, not black and white as many in the West see them. He is not a cold warrior; he is an intelligent man, a bit of a pragmatist, a good deal of an existentialist; he is prepared, as Pope John was, to look for the good elements in all systems.

And having lived through the Nazi holocaust he will need no telling that right-wing totalitarianism is every bit as much to be feared as left-wing. He knows the parallels between the Polish situation and that of Latin America, and he can make the mental leap into the other problem areas of the world; nor does he believe that Europe is the centre and mainspring of the world. 'By one of those instant elisions of opinion he has become thought of not just as a spiritual leader out of communism – "a man from the front-line made commander-in-chief", as one archbishop put it – but as a Pope for Africa, for Latin America, for Asia and for China as well,' proclaimed *The Economist*.[1] Or, as Christopher Booker so tellingly put it: 'John Paul II already seems to have placed the Roman Catholic Church back at the centre of the psychic drama of mankind in a way which even only a few weeks ago would have seemed inconceivable.'[2] That staunch faith which has withstood the on-slaughts of Nazis and Communists may well in itself be the greatest gift John Paul can bring to the service of the Church. He has the moral toughness of the survivor and the spiritual strength that only survival against the odds can provide.

With a passion for freedom matched by a passion for man's humanity, he sees that the materialism which threatens them both is common to all industrialised nations whether of East or West. The hedonism, violence, triviality and growing barbarism of Western society saddens him and he understands how hard it is to keep the faith amid so many pressures.

And what of Euro-communism, the new breed spawned in the industrial jungles of the West? The Cardinals, so many of them Italian, could not have been unaware of that problem when they elected this Pope. Will John Paul, now Bishop of Rome, be able to deal with the crisis that threatens to overwhelm that city? All that can be said is that he will act with prudence and forethought rather than prejudice. As a leading article in *The Times* put it: 'The Polish Church has not been one of reaction. It has led the Poles to regard Russia with prudence and Germany with reconciliation.' Between these two extremes there surely lie some grounds for hope.

In any case, it is good that the head of the Church and the Bishop of Rome should no longer be an Italian. The Popes of this century – with the solitary and extra-ordinary exception of John XXIII – have been obsessed with Italian politics, to the point of being diminished by them. Even Paul VI, whose concern for the world outside Italy was real, suffered from this Italian disease. The pronouncements he made, the encyclicals he wrote, were made by an Italian for Italians; and the universal Church was required to fit into this narrow straitjacket as best it could. John Paul cannot be so preoccupied. The immediate result of Vatican pressure may well be the loss of votes from Christian Democrats to Communists, but Italian politics cannot fail to be healthier as they become freer.

'We're back in the business of religion again,' a priest was heard to say on the Piazza of St Peter after the Pope's election. That seems to be the instinctive feeling. 'All of a sudden the Church has become catholic again,' said another. Catholic, universal, a Church that looks outward, a poor Church, a Church that knows how to suffer. The change in the air must have something to do with the personality of the man himself, and with the fact that suffering is etched into his face. 'Our Italian Cardinals are very nice people but none of them has ever seen the inside of a prison,' *Newsweek* reported a Roman diplomat as saying. And the same journal put its finger on the truth when it suggested:

> Wojtyla's great gift to the Church – in Africa and Asia as well as in Eastern Europe and Latin America – may be that he has restored the ancient image of the suffering servant to the see of St Peter. It is an image that has all but disappeared among the affluent Catholic communities of Western Europe and North America but it is the one that best reveals the spirit of Jesus Christ.

And lastly, what of the Roman Catholic Church itself? Will John Paul be able to reduce the tensions between those who want to de-centralise away from Rome and those who would centralise even more? Between those who wish for variety within unity, for national autonomous Churches which understand the needs of their own members yet fully understand that they belong (and are proud to belong) to a universal Church; and those who prefer orders delivered, *de haut en bas*, direct from Rome? Can he hold the balance between the traditionalists and progressives and prevent the wild men in both camps from over-reaching themselves? (At least it can be said that he has a record of tolerance, of being unwilling to condemn anyone out of hand. 'Let us wait a little longer,' he would say in Cracow, when asked to chastise an erring seminarian or priest.) Can he promote, as he has sworn to, the decrees of the Vatican Council and in particular the Dogmatic Constitution, *Lumen Gentium*, which re-defined the whole nature and purpose of the Church, without falling foul of those who still see the Church as a beleaguered fortress defending the deposit of faith against the onslaughts of the outside world? Will he be able to reform the Curia, the creaking, antique civil service of the Vatican? He has already shown signs that he will not be a rubber-stamp: although he eventually re-appointed the Heads of the various Vatican Congregations, he did not do so immediately, but only after he had interviewed them all at length. And it could be that the re-appointments will be temporary.

His commitment to collegiality – the sharing of authority between Pope and bishops – appears to be unshakeable. But there is a long way to go before it is achieved. The Church is still a monarchy, with the Pope at its head. For valid pastoral reasons, and not out of hunger for power, the bishops want a greater say in the life of the Church, a more deliberative less consultative role; and they do not want to be a second row of bureaucrats, merely there to implement Curial regulations. John Paul has shared their frustrations, but will he be able to effect the change?

On issues such as divorce, abortion and birth control he is bound to uphold the traditional teaching of the Church, but his recent writings and comments show that his mind is not closed to change, and in any case his approach to these subjects is pastoral rather than dogmatic. (Three years ago in his own diocese he offered help to any girl in distress. Since that time committees have been set up in every parish to give help to single mothers.) Would-be women priests are not likely to engage his support as yet, but then they have never been an issue in Poland, and he may prove more flexible than is thought. But he will not be going for any cheap or gimmicky changes and priests who trivialise what is important will not be popular with him. Neither will those who leave their ministries: the idea of sacrifice for one's beliefs is deeply ingrained in him, and the ideal of Maximilian Kolbe is always firmly before him.

Anxiously waiting to see if inter-communion has been brought any nearer by John Paul's accession, the non-Roman Christians are waiting in the wings. There will be problems there too, but he is committed to going forward and is deeply committed to the search for unity. He does not go back on commitments.

The problems which face him are immense, and the sheer

enormity and scope of the expectations to which his election has given birth may prove to be a grave handicap. Too much may be expected too quickly, and hopes left unfulfilled may sour rapidly to disillusionment. 'They have started the Church on a journey, the end of which cannot be known,' said an editorial in *The Times*. It is some comfort to know that the man in the driver's seat is neither a kerb-crawler nor a speed-maniac, but one who will study the route with care, take advice, drive with skill and intelligence tempered with prudence, be solicitous for the welfare of his passengers, and who, unlike most of the latter, has a good idea of where he is heading.

\*    \*    \*

'Pope of the Mountain People', they have called him, and that, after all, may explain much. The mountains gave him the passion for every kind of freedom, freedom subject to self-discipline; they developed in him the sturdy courage needed to overcome all obstacles; and they endowed him with serenity and balance. 'I would say,' commented George Williams, a Protestant theologian at Harvard and a friend of ten-years' standing, 'that in a most remarkable way he is a man whose soul is at leisure with itself.'[3]

A Polish philosopher, one of that select group who, at the installation ceremony, carried the label *Famigliari del Santo Padre* (close friends of the Holy Father), returned from Rome to Cracow and said with mingled pride and sorrow: 'Now at last he is where he ought to be. He is more truly himself than he has ever been.'

1. 21.10.78.
2. *Spectator*, 28.10.78.
3. *Newsweek*, 30.10.78.

# Bibliography

Andrzejewski, George, *Ashes and Diamonds*, Penguin.

Beeson, Trevor, *Discretion and Valour: Religious Conditions in Russia and Eastern Europe*, Collins Fount Paperbacks.

Fournier, Eva, *Poland*, Vista Books, London and New York, 1964.

Galter, Albert, *The Red Book of the Persecuted Church*, M. H. Gill & Son, 1957.

Hebblethwaite, Peter, *Year of Three Popes*, Collins, 1978.

Johnson, Paul, *Pope John XXIII*, Hutchinson.

Shirer, William L., *The Rise and Fall of The Third Reich*, Pan Books.

Wojtyla, Karol, *Segno di Contraddizione*, Vita e Pensiero, Cath. University of Milan, 1977.

*On Human Life: an examination of Humanae Vitae*, Burns & Oates.

*Dissent in Poland 1976–77* – reports and documents published by the Association of Polish Students in Exile.